Mmmm...
Soup

Mmmm...
Soup

First published in 2011

LOVE FOOD is an imprint of Parragon Books Ltd

Parragon
Queen Street House
4 Queen Street
Bath BA1 1HE, UK

ISBN: 978-1-4454-2446-0

Printed in China

Cover photography by Mike Cooper
Food Styling by Lincoln Jefferson
Internal design by Talking Design
Introduction by Linda Doeser

Notes for the Reader
This book uses imperial, metric, and US cup measurements. Follow the same units of measurement
throughout; do not mix imperial and metric. All spoon measurements are level: teaspoons are assumed to
be 5 ml, and tablespoons are assumed to be 15 ml. Unless otherwise stated, milk is assumed to be whole,
eggs and individual vegetables, such as potatoes, are medium, and pepper is freshly ground
black pepper.

The times given are an approximate guide only. Preparation times differ according to the techniques used
by different people and the cooking times may also vary from those given as a result of the type of oven
used. Optional ingredients, variations, or serving suggestions have not been included in the calculations.

Recipes using raw or very lightly cooked eggs should be avoided by infants, the elderly, pregnant women,
convalescents, and anyone with a chronic condition. Pregnant and breast-feeding women are advised
to avoid eating peanuts and peanut products. People with nut allergies should be aware that some of
the prepared ingredients used in the recipes in this book may contain nuts. Always check the packaging
before use.

contents

introduction

Homemade soup is the ultimate comfort food, yet it is one of the easiest dishes to make. Its versatility is almost endless as it may be based on vegetables, meat, poultry, fish, or shellfish. Some soups are delicately flavored and elegant, while others are robust and substantial. Chilled soups are a delightful summer treat and nothing is more welcome on a cold winter's evening than a steaming bowl of homemade broth.

The basis of a really flavorsome soup is a good stock. Time is at a premium in this modern world and, fortunately, there are some good-quality store-bought stocks available. Bouillon cubes are convenient and keep for reasonably a long time, but they are often very salty. Price is a guide, although not invariably, to their quality. Liquid stocks and concentrates often have a better flavor and the best ones have no additives or salt.

Making your own stock isn't difficult but is time-consuming. Life is too short for nonprofessional cooks to saw and roast beef bones, bring them slowly to a boil with vegetables—about 1 hour—and then simmer for anything up to 3 hours, before skimming and straining, then clarifying the next day. However, there are some shortcuts that will produce a very acceptable stock to enhance the flavor of homemade soups without your spending hours in the kitchen.

Many grocery stores sell stock or stew packs containing chicken wings, onion, carrot, and sometimes other vegetables, such as leeks. Put one or two of these into a large pan, depending on how much stock you require, add any extra vegetables if you like, and a bouquet garni, and pour in water to cover by about 2 inches/5 cm. Bring to a boil over low heat, skimming off any foam that rises to the surface, then simmer gently, uncovered and without stirring, for 1–2 hours. Strain through a cheesecloth-lined strainer into a bowl, then ideally chill in the refrigerator overnight, and spoon off the fat that will have set on the surface the next day. If you want to use the stock immediately, blot up the globules of fat from the surface with paper towels. You can also make a chicken stock in the same way using the carcass and trimmings from a roast chicken and a selection of vegetables, such as onion, leek, carrots, celery stalks, and even lettuce.

Mmmm...

You can make a quick beef stock with 1 lb 2 oz/500 g ground beef, a diced carrot, leek, onion, and celery stalk, and some fresh herb sprigs, such as parsley. Put them into a pan, pour in 5⅔ cups water, and bring to a boil over low heat, skimming off any scum that rises to the surface. Partially cover the pan and simmer gently, without stirring, for 1 hour, then strain as above and remove the fat.

An easy vegetable stock can be made by gently cooking a chopped onion, carrot, and celery stalk, plus any other vegetables you have at hand in 4 tablespoons of butter for 10 minutes. Add some fresh herb sprigs, such as thyme and parsley, pour in 4 cups of water, and bring to a boil. Partially cover the pan and simmer gently for 20 minutes. Strain into a bowl.

Vegetable trimmings, such as asparagus stalks and the outer leaves of cauliflower, and cooking water, such as that used for green beans or corncobs, can be added to the stockpot. However, it is best to avoid strong-tasting brassicas, such as cabbage and Brussels sprouts.

Do not season the stock until you are using it to make soup, as salt may become concentrated during cooking, thus spoiling the flavor, and pepper tends to make it cloudy.

Embellishments & accompaniments

- Turn your soup into something special with a dash of wine or fortified wine, such as sherry, Madeira, or Marsala. Add it just before serving for extra flavor and aroma. If you want to cook out the alcohol but retain the flavor, let the soup bubble for a couple of minutes before serving.

- A sprinkling of chopped fresh herbs or finely grated Parmesan makes an easy garnish and a spoonful of pesto is a great addition to minestrone.

- A swirl of heavy cream, plain yogurt, or crème fraîche looks very attractive in a colorful creamy vegetable soup.

- A sprinkling of caviar or—much less expensive—keta or salmon roe makes a sophisticated garnish for a special fish or shellfish soup.

- For an unusual vegetable garnish, slice 2 carrots into very fine julienne strips and put them into a pan. Add water to cover and 2 tablespoons of butter. Bring to a boil, then reduce the heat and simmer for about 5 minutes, until tender but still firm to the bite. Drain well.

- Croutons are a great addition to soups. Cut 2 thick crustless slices of white bread into ¼-inch/5-mm cubes or, for a special occasion, diamonds, triangles, or batons. Heat 4 tablespoons of butter or 2 tablespoons of olive or sunflower oil in a skillet, add the bread, and cook, tossing and stirring constantly, for a few minutes, until golden brown all over. Remove with a slotted spoon and drain on paper towels. For garlic croutons, cook a peeled whole garlic clove in the pan for 1–2 minutes, until lightly browned, then remove before adding the bread.

- Fresh bread and rolls are a traditional accompaniment to soup. Most grocery stores sell a huge range, including ciabatta and focaccia—perfect for Italian soups—brioche and baguettes—great for all kinds of soups, particularly French ones—corn bread—ideal for chowders—and, of course, whole wheat, white, soda bread, and seeded rolls.

crusty white bread

makes 1 medium loaf

- 1 egg
- 1 egg yolk
- ¾–1 cup lukewarm water
- 4½ cups white bread flour, plus extra for dusting
- 1½ tsp salt
- 2 tsp superfine sugar
- 1 tsp active dry yeast
- 2 tbsp butter, diced
- vegetable oil, for brushing

1 Lightly beat together the egg and egg yolk in a measuring cup. Stir in enough lukewarm water to make up to 1¼ cups.

2 Sift the flour and salt together into a bowl and stir in the sugar and yeast. Add the butter and rub it in with your fingertips until the mixture resembles breadcrumbs. Make a well in the center add the egg mixture, and work to a smooth dough. Turn out onto a lightly floured counter and knead well for 10 minutes, until smooth.

3 Brush a bowl with oil. Shape the dough into a ball, put it into the bowl, and put the bowl into a plastic bag or cover with a damp dish towel. Let rise in a warm place for 1–2 hours, until the dough has doubled in volume.

4 Brush a 7¼ x 4½ x 3½-inch/19 x 12 x 9-cm loaf pan with oil. Turn out the dough onto a lightly floured counter, punch down with your fist, and knead for 1 minute. Shape the dough the same length of the pan and three times the width. Fold it lengthwise into 3 and place in the pan, seam side down. Put the pan into a plastic bag or cover with a damp dish towel and let rise in a warm place for 30 minutes, until the dough has reached the top of the pan.

5 Preheat the oven to 425°F/220°C. Bake the loaf for 30 minutes, until it has shrunk from the sides of the pan, is golden brown, and sounds hollow when tapped on the bottom with your knuckles. Turn out onto a wire rack to cool.

whole wheat bread

makes 1 small loaf
- 2 cups whole wheat bread flour, plus extra for dusting
- 1 tsp salt
- 1 tbsp nonfat dry milk
- 2 tbsp brown sugar
- 1 tsp active dry yeast
- 1½ tbsp vegetable oil, plus extra for brushing
- ¾ cup lukewarm water

1 Sift the flour and salt together into a bowl, add the bran from the sifter, and stir in the milk, sugar, and yeast. Make a well in the center and pour in the oil and lukewarm water. Stir well with a wooden spoon until the dough begins to come together, then knead with your hands until it leaves the side of the bowl. Turn out onto a lightly floured counter and knead well for about 10 minutes, until smooth and elastic.

2 Brush a bowl with oil. Shape the dough into a ball, put it into the bowl, and put the bowl into a plastic bag or cover with a damp dish towel. Let rise in a warm place for 1 hour, until the dough has doubled in volume.

3 Brush a 6½ x 4¼ x 3¼-inch/17 x 11 x 8-cm loaf pan with oil. Turn out the dough onto a lightly floured counter, punch down with your fist, and knead for 1 minute. With lightly floured hands, shape the dough into a rectangle the same length as the pan and flatten slightly. Fold it lengthwise into 3 and place in the prepared pan, seam side down. Put the pan into a plastic bag or cover with a damp dish towel and let rise in a warm place for 30 minutes, until the dough has reached the top of the pan.

4 Preheat the oven to 425°F/220°C. Bake the loaf for about 30 minutes, until it has shrunk from the sides of the pan, the crust is golden brown, and it sounds hollow when tapped on the bottom with your knuckles. Turn out onto a wire rack to cool.

Mmmm...
vegetables

fresh tomato soup with pasta

serves 4
- 1 tbsp olive oil
- 4 large plum tomatoes
- 1 onion, cut into quarters
- 1 garlic clove, thinly sliced
- 1 celery stalk, coarsely chopped
- generous 2 cups chicken stock
- 2 oz/55 g dried soup pasta
- salt and pepper
- chopped fresh flat-leaf parsley, to garnish

1 Pour the oil into a large heavy-bottom saucepan and add the tomatoes, onion, garlic, and celery. Cover and cook over low heat, occasionally shaking gently, for 45 minutes, until pulpy.

2 Transfer the mixture to a food processor or blender and process to a smooth puree.

3 Push the puree through a strainer into a clean saucepan.

4 Add the stock and bring to a boil. Add the pasta, bring back to a boil, and cook for 8–10 minutes, until the pasta is tender but still firm to the bite. Season with salt and pepper to taste.

5 Ladle into warmed bowls, sprinkle with parsley, and serve immediately.

italian tomato soup

serves 6

- 10½ oz/300 g sourdough bread
- generous ⅓ cup chicken stock
- 4 tbsp extra virgin olive oil
- 3 tbsp fresh sage leaves, shredded
- 4 garlic cloves, peeled and finely chopped
- 1 lb 12 oz/800 g canned peeled plum tomatoes
- 1 tsp sugar
- 1 cup hot water
- ½ cup grated Parmesan cheese
- salt and pepper

1 Chop the bread into rough chunks, about 1 inch/2.5 cm square. Place a heavy-bottom saucepan over medium heat. Add the stock, oil, and sage and simmer until reduced by half. Add the bread and garlic, increase the heat to high, and fry until all the liquid has been soaked up and the bread begins to become crispy.

2 Add the tomatoes and sugar, stir, and simmer for 15 minutes. Add hot water to thin the soup to your preferred consistency (it should be thick). Simmer for an additional minute. Taste and adjust the seasoning.

3 Ladle into bowls, sprinkle a little Parmesan cheese on top, and serve immediately.

tomato & white bean soup

serves 6

- 3 tbsp olive oil
- 1⅔ cups chopped red onions
- 1 celery stalk with leaves, chopped
- 1 red bell pepper, seeded and chopped
- 2 garlic cloves, finely chopped
- 4 cups peeled and chopped plum tomatoes
- 5⅔ cups vegetable stock
- 2 tbsp tomato paste
- 1 tsp sugar
- 1 tbsp sweet paprika
- 1 tbsp butter
- 1 tbsp all-purpose flour
- 14 oz/400 g canned cannellini beans, drained and rinsed
- salt and pepper
- 3 tbsp chopped fresh flat-leaf parsley, to garnish

1 Heat the olive oil in a large pan. Add the onions, celery, bell pepper, and garlic and cook over low heat, stirring occasionally, for 5 minutes, until softened.

2 Increase the heat to medium, add the tomatoes, and cook, stirring occasionally, for an additional 5 minutes, then pour in the vegetable stock. Stir in the tomato paste, sugar, and sweet paprika and season to taste with salt and pepper. Bring to a boil, reduce the heat, and simmer for 15 minutes.

3 Meanwhile, mash together the butter and flour to a paste in a small bowl with a fork. Stir the paste, in small pieces at a time, into the soup. Make sure each piece is fully incorporated before adding the next.

4 Add the beans, stir well, and simmer for another 5 minutes, until heated through. Sprinkle with the parsley and serve immediately.

minestrone

serves 4

- 2 tbsp olive oil
- 2 garlic cloves, chopped
- 2 red onions, chopped
- 1 red bell pepper, seeded and chopped
- 1 orange bell pepper, seeded and chopped
- 14 oz/400 g canned chopped tomatoes
- 4 cups vegetable stock
- 1 celery stalk, trimmed and sliced
- 14 oz/400 g canned cranberry beans, drained
- 1 cup shredded green leafy cabbage
- ½ cup frozen peas, thawed
- 1 tbsp chopped fresh parsley
- 2¾ oz/75 g dried vermicelli
- salt and pepper
- freshly grated Parmesan cheese, to garnish

1 Heat the oil in a large saucepan over medium heat, add the garlic and onions, and cook, stirring, for 3 minutes, until slightly softened. Add the red and orange bell peppers and the chopped tomatoes and cook for an additional 2 minutes, stirring. Stir in the stock, then add the celery, cranberry beans, cabbage, peas, and parsley. Season with salt and pepper to taste. Bring to a boil, then lower the heat and simmer for 30 minutes.

2 Add the vermicelli to the pan. Cook for another 10–12 minutes, or according to the directions on the package. Remove from the heat and ladle into serving bowls. Garnish with freshly grated Parmesan and serve immediately.

black bean soup

serves 6

- 3 tbsp corn oil
- 1 large onion, chopped
- 2 celery stalks, chopped
- 2 garlic cloves, chopped
- 2½ cups dried black beans or black-eyed peas, soaked overnight in cold water to cover, and drained
- 11¼ cups vegetable stock
- ¾ tsp cayenne pepper
- 5 tbsp lemon juice
- 2 tbsp red wine vinegar
- 2 tbsp dry sherry
- 4 hard-cooked eggs, coarsely chopped
- salt and pepper
- chopped celery leaves, to garnish
- grated cheddar cheese, to serve

1 Heat the oil in a large pan. Add the onion, celery, and garlic and cook over low heat, stirring occasionally, for 6–8 minutes, until softened.

2 Increase the heat to medium, add the beans, pour in the vegetable stock, and bring to a boil. Reduce the heat, cover, and simmer for 2–2½ hours, until the beans are tender.

3 Remove the pan from the heat and let cool slightly. Ladle all or half the soup, depending on the texture you require, into a food processor or blender, and process to a puree.

4 Return the soup to the pan and bring just to a boil. If it is very thick, add a little more stock or water. Stir in the cayenne, lemon juice, vinegar, sherry, and hard-cooked eggs and season to taste with salt and pepper. Reduce the heat and simmer, stirring constantly, for 10 minutes.

5 Remove the pan from the heat and ladle the soup into warmed bowls. Garnish with celery leaves and serve immediately, sprinkled with grated cheddar cheese.

traditional bean & cabbage soup

serves 6

- generous 1 cup dried cannellini beans, soaked overnight and drained
- 3 tbsp olive oil
- 2 red onions, coarsely chopped
- 4 carrots, sliced
- 4 celery stalks, coarsely chopped
- 4 garlic cloves, coarsely chopped
- 2½ cups vegetable stock
- 14 oz/400 g canned chopped tomatoes
- 2 tbsp chopped fresh flat-leaf parsley
- 1 lb 2 oz/500 g black kale or savoy cabbage, thinly sliced
- 1 small 2-day-old ciabatta loaf, torn into small pieces
- salt and pepper
- extra virgin olive oil, to serve

1 Place the beans in a large saucepan. Cover with cold water and bring to a boil, skimming off any foam. Reduce the heat and simmer, uncovered, for 1–1½ hours, until tender.

2 Meanwhile, heat the olive oil in a large saucepan, add the onions, carrots, and celery, and cook over medium heat for 10–15 minutes, until softened. Add the garlic and cook for 1–2 minutes.

3 Drain the beans, reserving the cooking water, and add half the beans to the pan. Add the stock, tomatoes, and parsley. Season with salt and pepper to taste.

4 Bring to a simmer and cook, uncovered and stirring occasionally, for 30 minutes. Add the cabbage and cook, stirring occasionally, for an additional 15 minutes.

5 Put the remaining beans in a food processor or blender with a little of the reserved cooking water and process to a smooth paste. Add to the soup.

6 Stir in the bread and add a little more water, if needed. The consistency should be thick. Serve immediately, drizzled with a little olive oil.

tuscan bean soup

serves 6

- 10½ oz/300 g canned cannellini beans, drained and rinsed
- 10½ oz/300 g canned cranberry beans, drained and rinsed
- 2½ cups chicken or vegetable stock
- 4 oz/115 g dried conchigliette or other small pasta shapes
- 4 tbsp olive oil
- 2 garlic cloves, finely chopped
- 3 tbsp chopped fresh flat-leaf parsley
- salt and pepper

1 Place half the cannellini and half the cranberry beans in a food processor or blender with half the stock and process until smooth. Pour into a large, heavy-bottom pan and add the remaining beans. Stir in enough of the remaining stock to achieve the consistency you like, then bring to a boil.

2 Add the pasta and return to a boil, then reduce the heat and cook for 15 minutes, or until tender.

3 Meanwhile, heat 3 tablespoons of the oil in a small skillet. Add the garlic and cook, stirring constantly, for 2–3 minutes, or until golden. Stir the garlic into the soup with the parsley.

4 Season to taste with salt and pepper and ladle into warmed soup bowls. Drizzle with the remaining oil and serve immediately.

squash & lentil soup

serves 6
- 3 tbsp olive oil
- 2 large onions, chopped
- 2 garlic cloves, chopped
- 2 tsp ground cumin
- 1 tsp ground cinnamon
- ½ tsp freshly grated nutmeg
- ½ tsp ground ginger
- ½ tsp ground coriander
- 2 lb 4 oz/1 kg butternut squash or pumpkin, seeded and cut into small chunks
- 1½ cups red or yellow lentils
- 7½ cups vegetable stock
- 3 tbsp lemon juice
- salt and pepper
- strained plain yogurt, to garnish

1 Heat the oil in a large pan. Add the onions and garlic and cook over low heat, stirring occasionally, for 5 minutes, until softened. Add the cumin, cinnamon, nutmeg, ginger, and coriander and cook, stirring constantly, for 1 minute.

2 Stir in the butternut squash and lentils and cook, stirring constantly for 2 minutes, then pour in the vegetable stock, and bring to a boil over medium heat. Reduce the heat and simmer, stirring occasionally, for 50–60 minutes, until the vegetables are tender.

3 Remove from the heat and let cool slightly, then ladle into a food processor or blender, and process to a smooth puree.

4 Return the soup to the rinsed-out pan, stir in the lemon juice, season to taste with salt and pepper, and reheat gently. Ladle into warmed bowls, top with a swirl of strained plain yogurt, and serve.

gazpacho

serves 4

- 1 red bell pepper, cored, seeded, and chopped
- 2 lb 4 oz/1 kg ripe tomatoes, cored and chopped
- 2 tbsp very finely chopped onion
- 3 garlic cloves, crushed
- 1 cucumber, peeled and chopped
- 3½ slices stale bread, crumbled
- 3 tbsp red wine vinegar or sherry vinegar
- 3½ tbsp olive oil, plus extra for drizzling
- ice cubes (optional)
- salt and pepper

1 Set aside a handful of the red bell pepper, a handful of the tomatoes, and half the chopped onion in the refrigerator. Put the rest in a food processor or blender with the garlic and cucumber, and puree until smooth. Add the bread, vinegar, and oil and blend again. Season with salt and pepper to taste. If the soup is too thick, add some ice, then place in the refrigerator for 2 hours.

2 When ready to serve, check the vinegar and seasoning and ladle into bowls. Scatter over the reserved red bell pepper, tomatoes, and onions, then drizzle over a swirl of olive oil. Serve immediately.

french onion soup

serves 6

- 1 lb 8 oz/675 g onions
- 3 tbsp olive oil
- 4 garlic cloves,
  3 chopped and 1 halved
- 1 tsp sugar
- 2 tsp chopped fresh thyme,
  plus extra sprigs to garnish
- 2 tbsp all-purpose flour
- ½ cup dry white wine
- 8½ cups vegetable stock
- 6 slices French bread
- 3 cups grated Gruyère
  cheese

1 Thinly slice the onions. Heat the oil in a large, heavy-bottom pan over medium–low heat, add the onions, and cook, stirring occasionally, for 10 minutes, or until they are just beginning to brown. Stir in the chopped garlic, sugar, and chopped thyme, then reduce the heat and cook, stirring occasionally, for 30 minutes, or until the onions are golden brown.

2 Sprinkle in the flour and cook, stirring constantly, for 1–2 minutes. Stir in the wine. Gradually stir in the stock and bring to a boil, skimming off any foam that rises to the surface, then reduce the heat and simmer for 45 minutes.

3 Meanwhile, preheat the broiler to medium. Toast the bread on both sides under the broiler, then rub the toast with the cut edges of the halved garlic clove.

4 Ladle the soup into 6 ovenproof bowls set on a baking sheet. Float a piece of toast in each bowl and divide the grated cheese among them. Place under the broiler for 2–3 minutes, or until the cheese has just melted. Garnish with thyme sprigs and serve immediately.

green vegetable soup

serves 6

- generous 6¾ cups vegetable stock
- 3 tablespoons olive oil
- 2 leeks, white parts only, chopped
- 2 tbsp all-purpose flour
- 1 tsp dried thyme
- ½ tsp fennel seeds
- 1 Boston lettuce, coarsely chopped
- 1 lb 2 oz/500 g spinach, coarse stalks removed
- 2½ cups shelled fresh or frozen peas
- 1 bunch of watercress or arugula
- 4 tbsp chopped fresh mint
- salt and pepper
- 2 tbsp chopped fresh parsley, to garnish
- garlic and herb bread, to serve

1 Pour the vegetable stock into a pan and bring to a boil. Meanwhile, heat the oil in a large pan. Add the leeks and cook over low heat, stirring occasionally, for 5 minutes, until softened, then remove the pan from the heat.

2 Stir in the flour until fully incorporated, then gradually stir in the hot stock, a little at a time. Season with salt and pepper to taste and add the thyme and fennel seeds.

3 Return the pan to the heat and bring to a boil, stirring constantly. Add the lettuce, spinach, peas, watercress, and mint and bring back to a boil. Boil, stirring constantly, for 3–4 minutes, then reduce the heat, cover, and simmer gently for 30 minutes.

4 Remove the soup from the heat and let cool slightly. Ladle it into a food processor or blender and process to a smooth puree. Return the soup to the rinsed-out pan and reheat, stirring occasionally. When it is piping hot, ladle into warmed bowls, sprinkle with the parsley, and serve immediately with garlic and herb bread.

cream of pea soup

serves 4
- 4 tbsp butter
- 1 onion, finely chopped
- 3 cups fresh or frozen peas
- ½ cup water
- 2½–3 cups milk
- salt and pepper

1 Melt the butter in a pan over low heat. Add the onion and cook, stirring occasionally, for 5 minutes, until softened.

2 Add the peas and pour in the water. Increase the heat to medium and simmer for 3–4 minutes, or until the peas are tender. (Frozen peas will be ready in 10 minutes.)

3 Add 2½ cups of the milk, season with salt and pepper to taste, and then bring to a boil, stirring continuously.

4 Remove the pan from the heat and let cool slightly, then pour the soup into a food processor or blender and process to a smooth puree.

5 Return the soup to the rinsed-out pan and bring back to a boil. If the soup seems too thick, heat the remaining milk in a small pan and stir it into the soup. Taste and adjust the seasoning, if necessary, and serve immediately.

watercress soup

serves 4

- 2 bunches of watercress (about 7 oz/200 g), thoroughly cleaned
- 3 tbsp butter
- 2 onions, chopped
- 1½ cups coarsely chopped potatoes
- 5 cups vegetable stock or water
- whole nutmeg, for grating (optional)
- salt and pepper
- ½ cup strained plain yogurt, or sour cream, to serve

1 Remove the leaves from the stalks of the watercress and set aside. Coarsely chop the stalks.

2 Melt the butter in a large saucepan over medium heat, add the onions, and cook for 4–5 minutes, until soft. Do not brown.

3 Add the potatoes to the saucepan and mix well with the onions. Add the watercress stalks and the stock.

4 Bring to a boil, then reduce the heat, cover, and simmer for 15–20 minutes, until the potato is soft.

5 Add the watercress leaves and stir in to heat through. Remove from the heat and transfer to a food processor or blender. Process until smooth and return the soup to the rinsed-out saucepan. Reheat and season with salt and pepper to taste, adding a good grating of nutmeg, if using.

6 Serve immediately in warmed bowls with the strained plain yogurt spooned on top and an extra grating of nutmeg, if desired.

asparagus soup

serves 4

- 15 oz/425 g canned asparagus spears
- 2 tbsp butter
- 2 tbsp all-purpose flour
- 2½ cups milk
- salt and pepper

1 Drain the asparagus, reserving the can juices. Cut the asparagus spears into short lengths and set aside.

2 Melt the butter in a pan over low heat. Stir in the flour and cook, stirring continuously, for 1 minute. Remove the pan from the heat.

3 Gradually stir in the reserved can juices, then slowly stir in the milk. Return the pan to the heat and bring to a boil, stirring continuously. Add the asparagus spears and heat through gently for 2 to 3 minutes.

4 Remove the pan from the heat and let cool slightly, then ladle the soup into a food processor and process until smooth. Stir well before ladling into bowls. Season with salt and pepper to taste, and serve immediately.

mushroom soup

serves 6

- 5 oz/140 g ciabatta or other rustic bread, crusts removed
- 4 tbsp butter
- 1 small onion, chopped
- 8½ cups coarsely chopped portobello mushrooms
- 1 garlic clove, finely chopped
- ½ tsp dried thyme
- ⅔ cup red wine or Madeira
- 4 cups vegetable stock
- salt and pepper

1 Tear the bread into pieces and put it into a bowl. Pour in cold water to cover and let soak for 10 minutes, then drain and squeeze out.

2 Meanwhile, melt the butter in a large pan. Add the onion and cook over low heat, stirring occasionally, for 8–10 minutes, until golden. Add the mushrooms and garlic and cook, stirring frequently, for 5–7 minutes, until they have released their liquid.

3 Add the bread and thyme and pour in the wine. Cook for 2 minutes, until the alcohol has evaporated, then pour in the vegetable stock and bring to a boil over medium heat. Reduce the heat, cover, and simmer for 20–25 minutes.

4 Remove the pan from the heat and let cool slightly. Transfer the soup to a food processor or blender, and process to a puree.

5 Return the soup to the rinsed-out pan, season to taste with salt and pepper, and reheat gently, stirring occasionally. Ladle into warmed bowls and serve immediately.

leek & potato soup

serves 4–6

- ¼ cup butter
- 1 onion, chopped
- 3 leeks, sliced
- 1½ cups ¾-inch/2-cm potato cubes
- 3½ cups vegetable stock
- salt and pepper
- 2 tbsp snipped fresh chives, to garnish
- ⅔ cup light cream, to serve (optional)

1 Melt the butter in a large saucepan over a medium heat, add the onion, leeks, and potatoes and sauté gently for 2–3 minutes, until softened but not browned. Pour in the stock, bring to a boil, then reduce the heat and simmer, covered, for 15 minutes.

2 Transfer the mixture to a food processor or blender and process until smooth. Return to the rinsed-out saucepan.

3 Reheat the soup, season with salt and pepper to taste, and serve immediately in warmed soup bowls, garnished with chives and swirled with the cream, if using.

potato & pasta soup with pesto

serves 4

- 1 lb/450 g floury potatoes
- 3 slices pancetta, chopped
- 2 tbsp olive oil
- 2¾ cups finely chopped onions
- 2½ cups chicken stock
- 2½ cups milk
- 3½ oz/100 g dried conchigliette or other small pasta shapes
- ⅔ cup heavy cream
- 2 tbsp chopped fresh flat-leaf parsley
- salt and pepper
- Parmesan cheese shavings, to serve immediately

pesto

- 1 cup fresh flat-leaf parsley leaves
- 2 garlic cloves, chopped
- generous ⅓ cup pine nuts
- 2 tbsp chopped fresh basil leaves
- ½ cup grated Parmesan cheese
- ⅔ cup olive oil

1 To make the pesto, put all of the ingredients in a food processor or blender and process for 2 minutes, or blend by hand using a mortar and pestle.

2 Peel the potatoes and finely chop.

3 Cook the pancetta in a large saucepan over medium heat for 4 minutes. Add the oil, potatoes, and onions and cook, stirring constantly, for 12 minutes.

4 Add the stock and milk to the pan, bring to a boil, and simmer for 10 minutes.

5 Add the pasta and simmer for an additional 10–12 minutes, or according to the cooking time given in the package directions.

6 Stir in the cream and simmer for 5 minutes. Add the chopped parsley and 2 tablespoons of the pesto. Season with salt and pepper to taste.

7 Ladle the soup into serving bowls and serve immediately with Parmesan shavings.

sweet potato & blue cheese soup

serves 4

- 4 tbsp butter
- 1 large onion, chopped
- 2 leeks, trimmed and sliced
- 1⅓ cups diced sweet potatoes
- 3½ cups vegetable stock
- 1 tbsp chopped fresh parsley
- 1 bay leaf
- ⅔ cup heavy cream
- 5½ oz/150 g blue cheese, crumbled
- pepper
- 2 tbsp finely crumbled blue cheese, to garnish
- thick slices of fresh bread, to serve

1 Melt the butter in a large pan over medium heat. Add the onion and leeks and cook, stirring, for about 3 minutes, until slightly softened. Add the sweet potatoes and cook for another 5 minutes, stirring, then pour in the stock, add the parsley and the bay leaf, and season to taste with pepper. Bring to a boil, then lower the heat, cover the pan, and simmer for about 30 minutes. Remove from the heat and let cool for 10 minutes. Remove and discard the bay leaf.

2 Transfer half of the soup into a food processor or blender and blend until smooth. Return to the pan with the rest of the soup, stir in the cream, and cook for another 5 minutes. Gradually stir in the crumbled cheese until melted (do not let the soup boil).

3 Remove from the heat and ladle into serving bowls. Garnish with finely crumbled cheese and serve with slices of fresh bread. Serve immediately.

broccoli & blue cheese soup

serves 6
- 3 tbsp butter
- 2 white onions, chopped
- 1 large potato, chopped
- 1 large head of broccoli, cut into small florets
- 6¾ cups vegetable stock
- 5½ oz/150 g blue cheese, diced
- pinch of ground mace
- salt and pepper
- croutons, to garnish (see page 9)

1 Melt the butter in a large pan. Add the onions and potato and stir well. Cover and cook over low heat for 7 minutes. Add the broccoli and stir well, then re-cover the pan and cook for an additional 5 minutes.

2 Increase the heat to medium, pour in the vegetable stock, and bring to a boil. Reduce the heat, season to taste with salt and pepper, re-cover, and simmer for 15–20 minutes, until the vegetables are tender.

3 Remove the pan from the heat, strain into a bowl, reserving the vegetables, and let cool slightly. Put the vegetables into a food processor or blender, add 1 ladleful of the stock, and process to a smooth puree. With the motor running, gradually add the remaining stock.

4 Return the soup to the rinsed-out pan and reheat gently until very hot but not boiling. Remove from the heat and stir in the cheese until melted and thoroughly combined. Stir in the mace and taste and adjust the seasoning, if necessary. Ladle into warmed bowls, sprinkle with the croutons, and serve immediately.

51

spinach &
cheese soup

serves 6-8

- 8 oz/225 g fresh baby spinach leaves, tough stalks removed
- 2½ cups milk
- 3 cups vegetable stock
- scant 1 cup cream cheese flavored with garlic and herbs
- salt and pepper
- croutons (see page 9)

1 Put the spinach in a large pan and pour in the milk and stock. Bring to a boil, then reduce the heat and simmer gently for 12 minutes. Remove the pan from the heat and let cool completely.

2 Ladle the cold soup into a food processor or blender, and process until smooth. Cut the cheese into chunks and add to the soup. Process again until smooth and creamy.

3 Pour the soup into a bowl and season with salt and pepper to taste. Cover with plastic wrap and let chill in the refrigerator for at least 3 hours. Stir well before ladling into bowls. Add croutons, and serve immediately.

53

miso soup

serves 4
- 4 cups water
- 2 tsp dashi granules
- 6 oz/175 g silken tofu, drained and cut into small cubes
- 4 shiitake mushrooms or white mushrooms, finely sliced
- 4 tbsp miso paste
- 2 scallions, chopped

1 Put the water in a large pan with the dashi granules and bring to a boil.

2 Add the tofu and mushrooms, reduce the heat, and let simmer for 3 minutes.

3 Stir in the miso paste and let simmer gently, stirring, until it has dissolved.

4 The miso paste will begin to settle, so stir the soup before serving to recombine.

5 Add the scallions and serve immediately.

hot & sour soup tom yum

serves 4

- 2 fresh red chiles, seeded and coarsely chopped
- 6 tbsp rice vinegar
- 5 cups vegetable stock
- 2 lemongrass stalks, halved
- 4 tbsp soy sauce
- 1 tbsp jaggery or brown sugar
- juice of ½ lime
- 2 tbsp peanut or vegetable oil
- 8 oz/225 g firm tofu, drained and cut into ½-inch/1-cm cubes
- 14 oz/400 g canned straw mushrooms, drained
- 4 scallions, chopped
- 1 small head of bok choy, shredded

1 Mix the chiles and vinegar together in a nonmetallic bowl, cover, and let stand at room temperature for 1 hour.

2 Meanwhile, bring the stock to a boil in a saucepan. Add the lemongrass, soy sauce, jaggery, and lime juice, reduce the heat, and simmer for 20–30 minutes.

3 Heat the oil in a preheated wok, add the tofu cubes, and stir-fry over a high heat for 2–3 minutes, or until browned all over. (You may need to do this in 2 batches, depending on the size of the wok.)

4 Remove with a slotted spoon and drain on paper towels.

5 Add the chiles and vinegar with the tofu, mushrooms, and half the scallions to the stock mixture and cook for 10 minutes.

6 Mix the remaining scallions with the bok choy.

7 Scatter over the scallions and bok choy and serve immediately.

mushroom &
ginger soup

serves 4

- ½ oz/15 g dried Chinese mushrooms or 4½ oz/125 g portobello or cremini mushrooms
- 4 cups vegetable stock
- 4½ oz/125 g thin egg noodles
- 2 tsp corn oil
- 3 garlic cloves, crushed
- 1-inch/2.5-cm piece fresh ginger, finely shredded
- 1 tsp light soy sauce
- 1¼ cups bean sprouts
- fresh cilantro leaves, to garnish

1 Soak the dried Chinese mushrooms for at least 30 minutes in 1¼ cups of the stock. Drain the mushrooms and reserve the stock. Remove the stems of the mushrooms and discard. Slice the caps and reserve.

2 Cook the noodles according to the directions on the package. Drain well, rinse under cold water, and drain again. Set aside.

3 Heat the oil in a preheated wok or large, heavy-bottom skillet over high heat. Add the garlic and ginger, stir, and add the mushrooms. Stir over high heat for 2 minutes.

4 Add the remaining stock with the reserved mushroom soaking liquid and bring to a boil. Add the soy sauce. Stir in the bean sprouts and cook until tender.

5 Divide the noodles among 4 serving bowls and ladle the soup on top. Garnish with cilantro leaves and serve immediately.

Mmmm...
meat

beef & tomato soup

serves 6
- 3 tbsp sunflower oil
- 1 onion, finely chopped
- 1 garlic clove, finely chopped
- 2 fresh red chiles, seeded and finely chopped
- 4 large tomatoes, peeled and chopped
- 1 lb 2 oz/500 g ground beef
- 2 carrots, diced
- 2 potatoes, diced
- 1–2 tbsp chopped fresh flat-leaf parsley, plus extra to garnish
- 5 cups beef stock
- salt and pepper
- crusty rolls, to serve

1 Heat the oil in a large pan. Add the onion and garlic and cook over low heat, stirring occasionally, for 5 minutes, until softened. Stir in the chiles and tomatoes and cook for an additional 5 minutes. Add the ground beef, increase the heat to medium, and cook, breaking it up with a wooden spoon, for 6–8 minutes, until lightly browned.

2 Stir in the carrots, potatoes, and parsley, pour in the stock, and season to taste with salt and pepper. Bring to a boil, then reduce the heat, cover, and simmer for 30 minutes, until the meat and vegetables are tender.

3 Taste and adjust the seasoning, adding salt and pepper if needed. Ladle the soup into warmed bowls, garnish with parsley, and serve immediately with crusty rolls.

beef & vegetable soup

serves 4

- ⅓ cup pearl barley
- 5 cups beef stock
- 1 tsp dried mixed herbs
- 8 oz/225 g lean sirloin or porterhouse steak
- 1 large carrot, diced
- 1 leek, shredded
- 1 medium onion, chopped
- 2 celery stalks, sliced
- salt and pepper
- 2 tbsp chopped fresh parsley, to garnish

1 Place the pearl barley in a large saucepan. Pour over the stock and add the mixed herbs. Bring to a boil, cover, and simmer gently over low heat for 10 minutes.

2 Meanwhile, trim any fat from the beef and cut the meat into thin strips.

3 Skim away any foam that has risen to the top of the stock with a flat ladle.

4 Add the beef, carrot, leek, onion, and celery to the pan. Bring back to a boil, cover, and simmer for about 1 hour, or until the pearl barley, beef, and vegetables are just tender.

5 Skim away any remaining foam that has risen to the top of the soup with a flat ladle. Blot the surface with absorbent paper towels to remove any fat. Adjust the seasoning according to taste.

6 Ladle the soup into warmed bowls, garnish with chopped parsley, and serve immediately.

ground beef & cilantro soup

serves 4–6

- 1 lb/450 g ground beef
- 6¼ cups chicken stock
- 3 egg whites, lightly beaten
- 1 tsp salt
- ½ tsp white pepper
- 1 tbsp finely chopped fresh ginger
- 1 tbsp finely chopped scallion
- 4–5 tbsp finely chopped cilantro, tough stems discarded

marinade

- 1 tsp salt
- 1 tsp sugar
- 1 tsp Chinese rice wine
- 1 tsp light soy sauce

1 Combine all the ingredients for the marinade in a bowl and marinate the beef for 20 minutes.

2 Bring the stock to a boil. Add the marinated beef, stirring to break up any clumps, and simmer for 10 minutes.

3 Slowly add the egg whites, stirring rapidly so that they form into fine shreds. Add the salt and pepper and taste to check the seasoning.

4 To serve, place the ginger, scallion, and cilantro in the bottom of individual bowls and pour the soup on top.

beef & bean soup

serves 4

- 2 tbsp vegetable oil
- 1 large onion, finely chopped
- 2 garlic cloves, finely chopped
- 1 green bell pepper, seeded and sliced
- 2 carrots, sliced
- 14 oz/400 g canned black-eyed peas
- 8 oz/225 g fresh ground beef
- 1 tsp each ground cumin, chili powder, and paprika
- ¼ head of cabbage, sliced
- 1¼ cups peeled, chopped tomatoes
- 2½ cups beef stock
- salt and pepper

1 Heat the oil in a large pan over medium heat. Add the onion and garlic and cook, stirring frequently, for 5 minutes, or until softened. Add the bell pepper and carrots and cook for an additional 5 minutes.

2 Meanwhile, drain the peas, reserving the liquid from the can. Place two-thirds of the peas, reserving the remainder, in a food processor or blender with the pea liquid and process until smooth.

3 Add the ground beef to the pan and cook, stirring constantly, to break up any lumps, until well browned. Add the spices and cook, stirring, for 2 minutes. Add the cabbage, tomatoes, stock, and pureed peas and season to taste with salt and pepper. Bring to a boil, then reduce the heat, cover, and let simmer for 15 minutes, or until the vegetables are tender.

4 Stir in the reserved peas, cover, and simmer for an additional 5 minutes. Ladle the soup into warmed soup bowls and serve immediately.

meat-in-a-bowl beef & herb soup

serves 6
- 2 onions
- 2 tbsp sunflower oil
- 1 tbsp ground turmeric
- 1 tsp ground cumin
- scant ½ cup green or yellow split peas
- 5 cups beef stock
- 8 oz/225 g ground beef
- 1 cup long-grain rice
- 1 tbsp chopped fresh cilantro
- 1 tbsp snipped fresh chives
- ⅔ cup finely chopped baby spinach
- 2 tbsp butter
- 2 garlic cloves, finely chopped
- 3 tbsp chopped fresh mint
- salt and pepper
- strained plain yogurt, to serve

1 Grate 1 of the onions into a bowl and finely chop the other. Heat the oil in a large pan. Add the chopped onion and cook over low–medium heat, stirring occasionally, for 8–10 minutes, until golden. Stir in the turmeric and cumin, add the split peas, and pour in the stock. Bring to a boil, then reduce the heat, cover, and simmer for 15 minutes.

2 Meanwhile, add the ground beef to the grated onion, season to taste with salt and pepper, and mix well. Shape the mixture into small balls with your hands.

3 Add the meatballs to the soup, re-cover the pan, and simmer for an additional 10 minutes. Add the rice and stir in the cilantro, chives, and spinach. Simmer, stirring frequently, for 25–30 minutes, until the rice is tender.

4 Melt the butter in a skillet. Add the garlic and cook over low heat, stirring frequently, for 2–3 minutes. Stir in the mint and cook for an additional minute.

5 Transfer the soup to warmed bowls and sprinkle over the garlic mixture. Serve immediately with yogurt.

beef goulash soup

serves 6

- 1 tbsp oil
- 1 lb 2 oz/500 g fresh lean ground beef
- 2 onions, finely chopped
- 2 garlic cloves, finely chopped
- 2 tbsp all-purpose flour
- 1 cup water
- 14 oz/400 g canned chopped tomatoes
- 1 carrot, finely chopped
- 1 large red bell pepper, roasted, peeled, seeded, and chopped
- 1 tsp Hungarian paprika
- ¼ tsp caraway seeds
- pinch of dried oregano
- 4 cups beef stock
- 2 oz/55 g tagliatelle, broken into small pieces
- salt and pepper
- sour cream and sprigs of fresh cilantro, to garnish

1 Heat the oil in a large wide saucepan over medium–high heat. Add the beef and sprinkle with salt and pepper. Cook until lightly browned.

2 Reduce the heat and add the onions and garlic. Cook for about 3 minutes, stirring frequently, until the onions are softened. Stir in the flour and continue cooking for 1 minute.

3 Add the water and stir to combine well, scraping the bottom of the pan to mix in the flour. Stir in the tomatoes, carrot, pepper, paprika, caraway seeds, oregano, and stock.

4 Bring just to a boil. Reduce the heat, cover, and simmer gently for about 40 minutes, stirring occasionally, until all the vegetables are tender.

5 Add the tagliatelle to the soup and simmer for an additional 20 minutes, or until the tagliatelle is cooked.

6 Taste the soup and adjust the seasoning, if necessary. Ladle into warmed bowls and top each with a tablespoonful of sour cream. Garnish with cilantro and serve immediately.

vietnamese beef soup

serves 2

- 5 cups good-quality beef stock
- 1 small fresh chile, chopped
- 1 cinnamon stick
- 2 star anise
- 2 cloves
- 8 oz/225 g porterhouse or tenderloin steak, cut into thin strips
- 10½ oz/300 g rice noodles
- 4 tbsp chopped fresh cilantro
- lime wedges, to garnish

1 Heat the stock, chile, and spices in a pan until boiling, then reduce the heat and simmer for about 5 minutes.

2 Add the beef strips and simmer for an additional 2–3 minutes until cooked to your liking.

3 Cook the noodles according to the package directions, then drain and place in 2 individual serving bowls.

4 Pour over the broth and sprinkle with chopped cilantro. Garnish with lime wedges and serve immediately.

chinese soup with meatballs

serves 4–6

- 5 dried Chinese mushrooms
- 12 oz/350 g ground beef
- 1 onion, finely chopped
- 1 garlic clove, finely chopped
- 1 tbsp cornstarch
- 1 egg, lightly beaten
- 3¾ cups beef stock
- ½ cup watercress, stalks removed
- 3 scallions, finely chopped
- 1–1½ tbsp soy sauce

1 Put the mushrooms into a bowl and pour in warm water to cover. Let soak for 15 minutes, then drain and squeeze dry. Discard the stalks and thinly slice the caps.

2 Mix together the ground beef, onion, garlic, cornstarch, and egg in a bowl until thoroughly combined. Shape the mixture into small balls, drop them into a bowl of ice water, and let stand for 15 minutes.

3 Pour the stock into a large pan and bring to a boil. Drain the meatballs well, add to the pan, and bring back to a boil. Reduce the heat and simmer for 10 minutes. Add the mushrooms, watercress, scallions, and soy sauce to taste and simmer for an additional 2 minutes. Serve immediately.

spicy beef & noodle soup

serves 4

- 4 cups beef stock
- ⅔ cup vegetable or peanut oil
- 3 oz/85 g rice vermicelli noodles
- 2 shallots, sliced thinly
- 2 garlic cloves, crushed
- 1-inch/2.5-cm piece fresh ginger, sliced thinly
- 8-oz/225-g piece beef tenderloin, cut into thin strips
- 2 tbsp Thai green curry paste
- 2 tbsp soy sauce
- 1 tbsp nam pla (fish sauce)
- chopped fresh cilantro, to garnish

1 Pour the stock into a large pan and bring to a boil. Meanwhile, heat the oil in a wok or large skillet. Add one-third of the noodles to the wok and cook for 10–20 seconds, until they have puffed up. Lift out with tongs, drain on paper towels, and set aside. Discard all but 2 tablespoons of the oil.

2 Add the shallots, garlic, and ginger to the wok and stir-fry for 1 minute. Add the beef and curry paste and stir-fry for an additional 3–4 minutes, until tender.

3 Add the beef mixture, the uncooked noodles, soy sauce, and fish sauce to the pan of stock and simmer for 2–3 minutes, until the noodles have swelled. Serve immediately, garnished with the chopped cilantro and the reserved crispy noodles.

mexican-style beef & rice soup

serves 4

- 3 tbsp olive oil
- 1 lb 2 oz/500 g boneless braising beef, cut into 1-inch/2.5-cm pieces
- ⅔ cup red wine
- 1 onion, finely chopped
- 1 green bell pepper, seeded and finely chopped
- 1 small fresh red chile, seeded and finely chopped
- 2 garlic cloves, finely chopped
- 1 carrot, finely chopped
- ¼ tsp ground coriander
- ¼ tsp ground cumin
- ⅛ tsp ground cinnamon
- ¼ tsp dried oregano
- 1 bay leaf
- grated rind of ½ orange
- 14 oz/400 g canned chopped tomatoes
- 5 cups beef stock
- ¼ cup long-grain white rice
- 3 tbsp raisins
- ½ oz/15 g semisweet chocolate, melted
- chopped fresh cilantro, to garnish

1 Heat half the oil in a large skillet over medium–high heat. Add the meat in one layer and cook until well browned, turning to color all sides. Remove the pan from the heat and pour in the wine.

2 Heat the remaining oil in a large saucepan over medium heat. Add the onion, cover, and cook for about 3 minutes, stirring occasionally, until just softened. Add the green bell pepper, chile, garlic, and carrot, and continue cooking, covered, for 3 minutes.

3 Add the coriander, cumin, cinnamon, oregano, bay leaf, and orange rind. Stir in the tomatoes and stock, along with the beef and wine. Bring almost to a boil, and when the mixture begins to bubble, reduce the heat to low. Cover and simmer gently, stirring occasionally, for about 1 hour, until the meat is tender.

4 Stir in the rice, raisins, and chocolate and continue cooking, stirring occasionally, for about 30 minutes until the rice is tender.

5 Ladle into warmed bowls and garnish with cilantro. Serve immediately.

taco soup

serves 4-6

- 1 tbsp sunflower oil
- 1 small onion, finely chopped
- 8 oz/225 g ground beef
- 14 oz/400 g canned chopped tomatoes
- 14 oz/400 g canned red kidney beans
- 1 cup tomato juice
- 1 tsp sugar
- ¼ tsp ground cinnamon
- ¼ tsp ground cumin
- 1 tsp chili powder
- 1½ cups beef stock
- 1 cup coarsely grated Monterey Jack or cheddar cheese
- 12 oz/350 g tortilla chips
- 1 cup sour cream
- 1 avocado
- 2 tbsp lemon juice

1 Heat the oil in a large pan. Add the onion and cook over low heat, stirring occasionally, for 5 minutes, until softened. Add the ground beef, increase the heat to medium, and cook, stirring frequently and breaking it up with a wooden spoon, for 8–10 minutes. Drain off as much fat as possible.

2 Stir in the tomatoes, kidney beans with their can juices, tomato juice, sugar, spices, and stock and bring to a boil. Reduce the heat, cover, and simmer, stirring occasionally, for 15 minutes.

3 Meanwhile, put the cheese, tortilla chips, and sour cream into separate serving dishes. Peel, pit, and dice the avocado and gently toss with the lemon juice.

4 Remove the soup from the heat and ladle into warmed bowls. Scatter the avocado over the soup and serve immediately with the cheese, tortilla chips, and sour cream.

pork & vegetable broth

serves 4

- 1 tbsp chili oil
- 1 garlic clove, chopped
- 3 scallions, sliced
- 1 red bell pepper, seeded and finely sliced
- 2 tbsp cornstarch
- 4 cups vegetable stock
- 1 tbsp soy sauce
- 2 tbsp rice wine or dry sherry
- 5½ oz/150 g pork tenderloin, sliced
- 1 tbsp finely chopped lemongrass
- 1 small red chile, seeded and finely chopped
- 1 tbsp grated fresh ginger
- 4 oz/115 g fine egg noodles
- 7 oz/200 g canned water chestnuts, drained and sliced
- salt and pepper

1 Heat the oil in a large pan. Add the garlic and scallions and cook over medium heat, stirring, for 3 minutes, until slightly softened. Add the bell pepper and cook for an additional 5 minutes, stirring.

2 In a bowl, mix the cornstarch with enough of the stock to make a smooth paste and stir it into the pan. Cook, stirring, for 2 minutes. Stir in the remaining stock and the soy sauce and rice wine, then add the pork, lemongrass, chile, and ginger. Season with salt and pepper to taste. Bring to a boil, then lower the heat and simmer for 25 minutes.

3 Bring a separate pan of water to a boil, add the noodles, and cook for 3 minutes, or according to the package directions. Remove from the heat, drain, then add the noodles to the soup along with the water chestnuts. Cook for another 2 minutes, then remove from the heat and ladle into serving bowls. Serve immediately.

salt pork & lentil soup

serves 6–8
- 8 oz/225 g salt pork, diced
- 2 tbsp olive oil
- 1 onion, chopped
- 3 garlic cloves, finely chopped
- 4 potatoes, diced
- 2¼ cups red lentils
- 8¾ cups vegetable stock
- 1 bouquet garni (1 bay leaf, 1 fresh thyme sprig, and 3 fresh parsley sprigs, tied together)
- salt and pepper

1 Put the salt pork into a large pan and cook over medium heat, stirring frequently, for 8–10 minutes, until it has released most of its fat and is browned all over. Remove from the pan with a slotted spoon and drain on paper towels. Set aside.

2 Add the oil to the pan and heat. Add the onion, garlic, and potatoes and cook over low heat, stirring occasionally, for 5 minutes, until the onion has softened. Stir in the lentils and cook, stirring constantly, for 5 minutes.

3 Pour in the vegetable stock, increase the heat to medium, add the bouquet garni, and bring to a boil, stirring constantly. Reduce the heat, cover, and simmer for 1½–2 hours, until the lentils are very soft. Stir in the salt pork, season with salt and pepper, if necessary, and cook, stirring occasionally, for another 10 minutes, until heated through.

4 Remove the pan from the heat. Remove and discard the bouquet garni. Pour the soup into warmed soup bowls and serve immediately.

split pea & ham soup

serves 6–8

- 2½ cups split green peas
- 1 tbsp olive oil
- 1 large onion, finely chopped
- 1 large carrot, finely chopped
- 1 celery stalk, finely chopped
- 4 cups chicken or vegetable stock
- 4 cups water
- 8 oz/225 g lean smoked ham, finely diced
- ¼ tsp dried thyme
- ¼ tsp dried marjoram
- 1 bay leaf
- salt and pepper

1 Rinse the peas under cold running water. Put in a saucepan and cover generously with water. Bring to a boil and boil for 3 minutes, skimming off the foam from the surface. Drain the peas.

2 Heat the oil in a large saucepan over medium heat. Add the onion and cook for 3–4 minutes, stirring occasionally, until just softened.

3 Add the carrot and celery and continue cooking for 2 minutes. Add the peas, pour over the stock and water, and stir to combine.

4 Bring just to a boil and stir the ham into the soup. Add the thyme, marjoram, and bay leaf. Reduce the heat, cover, and cook gently for 1–1½ hours, until the ingredients are very soft. Remove the bay leaf.

5 Taste and adjust the seasoning, adding salt and pepper to taste, if needed. Ladle into warmed soup bowls and serve immediately.

wonton soup

serves 6–8

- 8 cups chicken stock
- 2 tsp salt
- ½ tsp white pepper
- 2 tbsp finely chopped scallion
- 1 tbsp chopped cilantro leaves, to serve

wontons

- 6 oz/175 g ground pork, not too lean
- 8 oz/225 g shrimp, peeled, deveined, and chopped
- ½ tsp finely chopped fresh ginger
- 1 tbsp light soy sauce
- 1 tbsp Chinese rice wine
- 2 tsp finely chopped scallion
- pinch of sugar
- pinch of white pepper
- dash of sesame oil
- 30 square wonton wrappers
- 1 egg white, lightly beaten

1 For the wonton filling, mix together the pork, shrimp, ginger, soy sauce, rice wine, scallion, sugar, pepper, and sesame oil, and stir well until the texture is thick and pasty. Set aside for at least 20 minutes.

2 To make the wontons, place a teaspoon of the filling at the center of a wrapper. Brush the edges with a little egg white. Bring the opposite points toward each other and press the edges together, creating a flowerlike shape. Repeat with the remaining wrappers and filling.

3 To make the soup, bring the stock to a boil and add the salt and pepper. Boil the wontons in the stock for about 5 minutes, or until the wrappers begin to wrinkle around the filling.

4 To serve, put the scallion in individual bowls, then spoon in the wontons and soup and sprinkle with the cilantro. Serve immediately.

pork rib soup with pickled mustard greens

serves 6

- 1 tbsp peanut oil
- 3 garlic cloves, thinly sliced
- 5 cups vegetable stock
- 1 lb 2 oz/500 g pork spareribs
- 3 oz/85 g cellophane noodles
- 10 oz/280 g canned Thai pickled mustard greens or Chinese snow pickles, well rinsed and coarsely chopped
- 2 tbsp nam pla (fish sauce)
- ½ tsp sugar
- pepper
- 1 red and 1 green chile, seeded and thinly sliced, to garnish

1 Heat the oil in a small skillet or wok. Add the garlic and stir-fry for a few minutes, until golden. Transfer to a plate and set aside.

2 Pour the vegetable stock into a pan and bring to a boil over medium heat. Add the spareribs and bring back to a boil, then reduce the heat, cover, and simmer for 15 minutes, until tender.

3 Meanwhile, put the cellophane noodles into a bowl, pour in hot water to cover, and let soak for 10 minutes, until softened. Drain well.

4 Add the noodles and pickled greens to the soup and bring back to a boil. Stir in the nam pla and sugar, season to taste with pepper, and ladle into warmed bowls. Garnish with the garlic slices and red and green chiles and serve immediately.

sauerkraut & sausage soup

serves 6
- 2 tbsp butter
- 1 tbsp all-purpose flour
- 1 tbsp sweet paprika
- 8¾ cups vegetable stock
- 1 lb 7 oz/650 g sauerkraut, drained
- 1 lb 2 oz/500 g smoked pork sausages, cut into 1-inch/2.5-cm slices
- ⅔ cup sour cream
- salt and pepper

dumplings
- ¾ cup white bread flour, plus extra for dusting
- pinch of salt
- 1 extra large egg

1 Melt the butter in a large pan over low heat. Add the all-purpose flour and paprika and cook, stirring constantly, for 2 minutes, then remove the pan from the heat. Gradually stir in the vegetable stock, a little at a time, until fully incorporated and the mixture is smooth.

2 Return the pan to medium heat and bring to a boil, stirring constantly. Add the sauerkraut and sausages and season to taste with salt and pepper. Reduce the heat, cover, and simmer for 30 minutes.

3 Meanwhile, make the dumplings. Sift together the flour and salt into a bowl. Beat the egg in another bowl, then gradually beat in the dry ingredients, a little at a time. Turn out onto a floured surface and knead until smooth. Cover and let rest for 15 minutes.

4 Divide the dough into 6 pieces and roll into sausage shapes. Flour your hands, pinch off pieces of the dough, and add to the soup. Re-cover the pan and simmer for 5 minutes more. Remove the pan from the heat, stir in the sour cream, and serve immediately.

sausage & red cabbage soup

serves 4
- 2 tbsp olive oil
- 1 garlic clove, chopped
- 1 large onion, chopped
- 1 large leek, sliced
- 2 tbsp cornstarch
- 4 cups vegetable stock
- 2 large potatoes, sliced
- 7 oz/200 g skinless sausages, sliced
- 1⅔ cups chopped red cabbage
- 7 oz/200 g canned black-eyed peas, drained
- ½ cup heavy cream
- salt and pepper
- ground paprika, to garnish

1 Heat the oil in a large pan. Add the garlic and onion and cook over medium heat, stirring, for 3 minutes, until slightly softened. Add the leek and cook for another 3 minutes, stirring.

2 In a bowl, mix the cornstarch with enough stock to make a smooth paste, then stir it into the pan. Cook, stirring, for 2 minutes. Stir in the remaining stock, then add the potatoes and sausages. Season with salt and pepper to taste. Bring to a boil, then lower the heat and simmer for 25 minutes.

3 Add the red cabbage and black-eyed peas and cook for 10 minutes, then stir in the cream and cook for another 5 minutes. Remove from the heat and ladle into serving bowls. Garnish with ground paprika and serve immediately.

split pea & sausage soup

serves 6

- 6 oz/175 g boneless side of pork, cut into cubes
- 8¾ cups vegetable stock
- 1 onion, chopped
- 4 leeks, chopped
- 3 carrots, chopped
- 3 celery stalks, chopped
- 1 tart apple, peeled, cored, and chopped
- 1⅔ cups split peas, soaked overnight in cold water to cover, drained, and rinsed
- 1 bouquet garni (see page 86)
- 1 tbsp molasses
- 4 bockwurst, Wienerwurst, or frankfurters, cut into 1-inch/2.5-cm lengths
- 2 tbsp butter
- salt and pepper
- crusty rye bread, to serve

1 Put the pork into a large pan and pour in the vegetable stock. Add the onion, leeks, carrots, celery, apple, peas, bouquet garni, and molasses and bring to a boil. Using a slotted spoon, skim off any foam that rises to the surface, then reduce the heat, cover, and simmer, stirring occasionally, for 2 hours.

2 Season the soup to taste with salt and pepper and remove and discard the bouquet garni. Stir in the sausages and butter and simmer for another 5 minutes. Serve immediately with rye bread.

cheese & bacon soup

serves 4

- 2 tbsp butter
- 2 garlic cloves, chopped
- 1 large onion, sliced
- 9 oz/250 g smoked lean bacon, chopped
- 2 large leeks, trimmed and sliced
- 2 tbsp all-purpose flour
- 4 cups vegetable stock
- 3 cups chopped potatoes
- scant ½ cup heavy cream
- 3 cups grated cheddar cheese, plus extra to garnish
- salt and pepper

1 Melt the butter in a large pan over medium heat. Add the garlic and onion and cook, stirring, for 3 minutes, until slightly softened. Add the chopped bacon and leeks and cook for another 3 minutes, stirring.

2 In a bowl, mix the flour with enough stock to make a smooth paste and stir it into the pan. Cook, stirring, for 2 minutes. Pour in the remaining stock, then add the potatoes. Season to taste with salt and pepper. Bring the soup to a boil, then lower the heat and simmer gently for 25 minutes, until the potatoes are tender and cooked through.

3 Stir in the cream and cook for 5 minutes, then gradually stir in the cheese until melted. Remove from the heat and ladle into individual serving bowls. Garnish with grated cheddar cheese and serve immediately.

bacon & lentil soup

serves 4
- 1 lb/450 g thick, rindless smoked bacon strips, diced
- 1 onion, chopped
- 2 carrots, sliced
- 2 celery stalks, chopped
- 1 turnip, chopped
- 1 large potato, chopped
- generous 2¼ cups French green lentils
- 1 bouquet garni (see page 86)
- 4 cups water or chicken stock
- salt and pepper

1 Heat a large, heavy-bottomed pan or flameproof casserole. Add the bacon and cook over medium heat, stirring, for 4–5 minutes, or until the fat runs. Add the chopped onion, carrots, celery, turnip, and potato and cook, stirring frequently, for 5 minutes.

2 Add the lentils and bouquet garni and pour in the water. Bring to a boil, reduce the heat, and simmer for 1 hour, or until the lentils are tender.

3 Remove and discard the bouquet garni and season the soup to taste with pepper, and with salt if necessary. Ladle into warmed soup bowls and serve immediately.

brown lentil & pasta soup

serves 4

- 4 strips lean bacon, cut into small squares
- 1 onion, chopped
- 2 garlic cloves, crushed
- 2 celery stalks, chopped
- 1¾ oz/50 g dried farfallini (small pasta bows)
- 14 oz/400 g canned brown lentils, drained
- 5 cups vegetable stock
- 2 tbsp chopped fresh mint, plus extra sprigs to garnish

1 Place the bacon in a large skillet together with the onion, garlic, and celery. Cook for 4–5 minutes, stirring, until the onion is tender and the bacon is just beginning to brown.

2 Add the pasta to the skillet and cook, stirring, for 1 minute to coat the pasta in the fat.

3 Add the lentils and stock and bring to a boil. Reduce the heat and simmer for 12–15 minutes, or according the package directions, until the pasta is tender but still firm to the bite.

4 Remove the skillet from the heat and stir in the chopped fresh mint. Transfer the soup to warmed soup bowls, garnish with fresh mint sprigs, and serve immediately.

hearty winter broth

serves 4

- 1 tbsp vegetable oil
- 1 lb 2 oz/500 g lean neck of lamb
- 1 large onion, sliced
- 2 carrots, sliced
- 2 leeks, sliced
- 4 cups vegetable stock
- 1 bay leaf
- sprigs of fresh parsley
- ¼ cup pearl barley
- salt and pepper

1 Heat the vegetable oil in a large, heavy-bottom saucepan and add the pieces of lamb, turning them to seal and brown on both sides. Lift the lamb out of the pan and set aside until ready to use.

2 Add the onion, carrots, and leeks to the saucepan and cook gently for about 3 minutes.

3 Return the lamb to the saucepan and add the vegetable stock, bay leaf, parsley, and pearl barley. Bring the mixture in the pan to a boil, then reduce the heat. Cover and simmer for 1½ –2 hours.

4 Discard the parsley sprigs. Lift the pieces of lamb from the broth and let them cool slightly. Remove the bones and any fat and chop the meat. Return the lamb to the broth and reheat gently. Season to taste with salt and pepper.

5 It is advisable to prepare this soup a day ahead, then let it cool, cover, and refrigerate overnight. When ready to serve, remove and discard the layer of fat from the surface and reheat the soup gently. Ladle into warmed bowls and serve immediately.

mixed vegetable soup with lamb meatballs

serves 6
- 2 onions, finely chopped
- 1 small celeriac, diced
- ½ rutabaga, diced
- 3 carrots, diced
- 2 potatoes, diced
- 2 red bell peppers, seeded and diced
- 4 tomatoes, peeled, seeded, and chopped
- 1 cup shelled fresh or frozen peas
- 1 lemon, sliced
- generous 6¾ cups vegetable stock
- salt and pepper

lamb meatballs
- 12 oz/350 g ground lamb
- 3 tbsp chopped fresh flat-leaf parsley
- ⅓ cup medium-grain rice
- all-purpose flour, for dusting
- salt and pepper

1 Put the onions, celeriac, rutabaga, carrots, potatoes, bell peppers, tomatoes, peas, and lemon slices into a large pan, pour in the vegetable stock, and season to taste with salt and pepper. Bring to a boil, then reduce the heat, cover, and simmer for 25–30 minutes.

2 Meanwhile, make the meatballs. Combine the lamb, parsley, and rice in a bowl, kneading well until thoroughly mixed. Season to taste with salt and pepper. Break off pieces of the mixture, about the size of golf balls, and shape them into balls between the palms of your hand. Dust with flour, shaking off the excess.

3 Add the meatballs to the soup, re-cover the pan, and cook, stirring occasionally, for an additional 40–45 minutes. Serve immediately.

chunky potato & beef soup

serves 4
- 2 tbsp vegetable oil
- 8 oz/225 g lean braising steak, cut into strips
- 8 oz/225 g new potatoes, halved
- 1 carrot, diced
- 2 celery stalks, sliced
- 2 leeks, sliced
- 3½ cups beef stock
- 8 baby corn, sliced
- 1 bouquet garni (see page 86)
- 2 tbsp dry sherry
- salt and pepper
- chopped fresh parsley, to garnish

1 Heat the vegetable oil in a large pan. Add the strips of meat to the pan and cook for 3 minutes, turning constantly. Add the potatoes, carrot, celery, and leeks to the pan. Cook for an additional 5 minutes, stirring.

2 Pour the beef stock into the pan and bring to a boil. Reduce the heat until the liquid is simmering, then add the baby corn and the bouquet garni. Cook for an additional 20 minutes, or until cooked through.

3 Remove and discard the bouquet garni. Stir the dry sherry into the soup, then season to taste with salt and pepper.

4 Ladle the soup into warmed bowls, garnish with chopped parsley, and serve immediately.

lamb & lemon soup

serves 6
- ½ cup all-purpose flour
- 1 lb 2 oz/500 g boneless leg of lamb, cut into cubes
- 3 tbsp olive oil
- 5 cups vegetable stock
- 2 carrots, cut into chunks
- 2 onions, cut into quarters
- 1 tsp cayenne pepper
- 3 egg yolks
- 2 tbsp lemon juice
- salt and pepper
- flatbreads, to serve

to garnish
- 4 tbsp butter
- ½ tsp ground cinnamon
- 2 tsp sweet or hot paprika
- 3 tbsp chopped fresh mint

1 Put the flour into a plastic bag and season with salt and pepper. Add the cubes of lamb, a few at a time, seal the bag, and shake to coat. Shake off any excess.

2 Heat the oil in a large pan. Add the lamb and cook over medium heat, stirring frequently, for 8–10 minutes, until lightly browned all over. Pour in the vegetable stock and bring to a boil, skimming off the foam that rises to the surface.

3 Add the carrots, onions, and cayenne pepper, season to taste with salt and pepper, and bring back to a boil. Reduce the heat, cover, and simmer for 1½–2 hours, until the meat is tender.

4 For the garnish, melt the butter in a pan over very low heat or in a microwave-safe bowl in the microwave. Remove from the heat and stir in the cinnamon and paprika.

5 Beat the egg yolks with the lemon juice in a bowl. Remove the pan from the heat and whisk a ladleful of the hot soup into the egg mixture, then add it to the pan. Return the pan to very low heat and heat through, gently rotating the pan, for 1–2 minutes; do not let the soup boil.

6 Ladle the soup into warmed soup bowls, spoon the spiced melted butter over the top, sprinkle with the mint, and serve immediately, accompanied by flatbreads.

lamb & rice soup

serves 4

- 5½ oz/150 g lean lamb
- scant ¼ cup rice
- 3½ cups lamb stock
- 1 leek, sliced
- 1 garlic clove, thinly sliced
- 2 tsp light soy sauce
- 1 tsp rice wine vinegar
- 1 medium open-cap mushroom, thinly sliced
- salt

1 Using a sharp knife, trim any visible fat from the lamb and cut the meat into thin strips. Set aside until required.

2 Bring a large pan of lightly salted water to a boil and add the rice. Return to a boil, stir once, reduce the heat, and cook for 10–15 minutes, or according to the package directions, until tender. Drain the cooked rice, rinse under cold running water, drain again, and set aside.

3 Place the lamb stock in a large pan and bring to a boil. Add the lamb, leek, garlic, soy sauce, and rice wine vinegar, reduce the heat, cover, and let simmer for 10 minutes, or until the lamb is tender and cooked through.

4 Add the mushroom slices and cooked rice to the pan and cook for an additional 2–3 minutes, or until the mushrooms are completely cooked through.

5 Ladle the soup into warmed bowls and serve immediately.

middle eastern soup with harissa

serves 4
- 2 eggplants
- 3 tbsp olive oil
- 6 lamb shanks
- 1 small onion, chopped
- 1¾ cups chicken stock
- 8 cups water
- 2 large sweet potatoes, cut into chunks
- 2-inch/5-cm piece cinnamon stick
- 1 tsp ground cumin
- 2 tbsp chopped fresh cilantro

harissa
- 2 red bell peppers, roasted, peeled, seeded, and chopped
- ½ tsp coriander seeds, dry-roasted
- 1 oz/25 g fresh red chiles, chopped
- 2 garlic cloves, chopped
- 2 tsp caraway seeds
- olive oil
- salt

1 Preheat the oven to 400°F/200°C. Prick the eggplants, place on a baking sheet, and bake for 1 hour. When cool, peel and chop.

2 Heat the oil in a pan. Add the lamb and cook until browned. Add the onion, stock, and water. Bring to a boil. Reduce the heat and let simmer for 1 hour.

3 For the harissa, process the bell peppers, coriander seeds, chiles, garlic, and caraway seeds in a food processor. With the motor running, add enough oil to make a paste. Season with salt, then spoon into a jar. Cover with oil, seal, and chill.

4 Remove the shanks from the stock, cut off the meat, and chop. Add the sweet potatoes, cinnamon, and cumin to the stock, bring to a boil, cover, and simmer for 20 minutes. Discard the cinnamon and process the mixture in a food processor with the eggplant. Return to the pan, add the lamb and cilantro, and heat until hot. Serve immediately with the harissa.

spicy lamb soup with chickpeas & zucchini

serves 4-6

- 1–2 tbsp olive oil
- 1 lb/450 g lean boneless lamb, such as shoulder or neck, trimmed of fat and cut into ½-inch/1-cm cubes
- 1 onion, finely chopped
- 2–3 garlic cloves, crushed
- 5 cups water
- 14 oz/400 g canned chopped tomatoes
- 1 bay leaf
- ½ tsp dried thyme
- ½ tsp dried oregano
- ⅛ tsp ground cinnamon
- ½ tsp ground cumin
- ¼ tsp ground turmeric
- 1 tsp harissa (see page 116), or more to taste
- 14 oz/400 g canned chickpeas, rinsed and drained
- 1 carrot, diced
- 1 potato, diced
- 1 zucchini, quartered lengthwise and sliced
- ⅔ cup fresh or defrosted frozen peas
- sprigs of fresh mint or cilantro, to garnish

1 Heat 1 tablespoon of the oil in a large saucepan or cast-iron casserole over medium–high heat. Add the lamb, in batches if necessary, and cook evenly until browned on all sides, adding a little more oil if needed. Remove the meat with a slotted spoon when browned.

2 Reduce the heat and add the onion and garlic to the pan. Cook, stirring frequently, for 1–2 minutes.

3 Add the water and return all the meat to the pan. Bring just to a boil and skim off any foam that rises to the surface. Reduce the heat and stir in the tomatoes, bay leaf, thyme, oregano, cinnamon, cumin, turmeric, and harissa. Simmer for about 1 hour, or until the meat is very tender. Discard the bay leaf.

4 Stir in the chickpeas, carrot, and potato and simmer for 15 minutes. Add the zucchini and peas and continue simmering for 15–20 minutes, or until all the vegetables are tender.

5 Adjust the seasoning, adding more harissa, if desired. Ladle the soup into warmed bowls, garnish with mint or cilantro, and serve immediately.

asian lamb soup

serves 4

- 5½ oz/150 g lean, tender, boneless lamb, such as neck or leg
- 2 garlic cloves, very finely chopped
- 2 tbsp soy sauce
- 5 cups chicken stock
- 1 tbsp grated fresh ginger
- 2-inch/5-cm piece lemongrass, sliced into very thin rounds
- ¼ tsp chili paste, or to taste
- 6–8 cherry tomatoes, quartered
- 4 scallions, sliced finely
- ¼ cup halved bean sprouts
- 2 tbsp cilantro leaves
- 1 tsp olive oil

1 Trim all visible fat from the lamb and slice the meat thinly. Cut the slices into bite-size pieces. Spread the meat in one layer on a plate and sprinkle over the garlic and 1 tablespoon of the soy sauce. Let marinate, covered, for at least 10 minutes or up to 1 hour.

2 Put the stock in a saucepan with the ginger, lemongrass, remaining soy sauce, and the chili paste. Bring just to a boil, reduce the heat, cover, and simmer for 10–15 minutes.

3 When ready to serve the soup, drop the tomatoes, scallions, bean sprouts, and cilantro leaves into the stock.

4 Heat the oil in a skillet and add the lamb with its marinade. Stir-fry the lamb just until it is no longer red and divide among warmed bowls.

5 Ladle over the hot stock and serve immediately.

Mmmm...
poultry

cream of chicken soup

serves 4
- 3 tbsp butter
- 4 shallots, chopped
- 1 leek, sliced
- 1 lb/450 g skinless, boneless chicken breasts, chopped
- 2½ cups chicken stock
- 1 tbsp chopped fresh parsley
- 1 tbsp chopped fresh thyme, plus extra sprigs to garnish
- ½ cup heavy cream
- salt and pepper

1 Melt the butter in a large pan over medium heat. Add the shallots and cook, stirring, for 3 minutes, until slightly softened. Add the leek and cook for another 5 minutes, stirring. Add the chicken, stock, and herbs, and season to taste with salt and pepper. Bring to a boil, then lower the heat and simmer for 25 minutes, until the chicken is tender and cooked through. Remove from the heat and let cool for 10 minutes.

2 Transfer the soup into a food processor or blender and process until smooth. Return the soup to the rinsed-out pan and warm over low heat for 5 minutes.

3 Stir in the cream and cook for another 2 minutes, then remove from the heat and ladle into serving bowls. Garnish with sprigs of thyme and serve immediately.

chicken & potato soup with bacon

serves 4

- 1 tbsp butter
- 2 garlic cloves, chopped
- 1 onion, sliced
- 9 oz/250 g smoked lean bacon, chopped
- 2 large leeks, sliced
- 2 tbsp all-purpose flour
- 4 cups chicken stock
- 5⅓ cups chopped potatoes
- 7 oz/200 g skinless, boneless chicken breast, chopped
- 4 tbsp heavy cream
- salt and pepper
- cooked bacon and sprigs of fresh flat-leaf parsley, to garnish

1 Melt the butter in a large pan over medium heat. Add the garlic and onion and cook, stirring, for 3 minutes, until slightly softened. Add the chopped bacon and leeks and cook for another 3 minutes, stirring.

2 In a bowl, mix the flour with enough stock to make a smooth paste and stir it into the pan. Cook, stirring, for 2 minutes. Pour in the remaining stock, then add the potatoes and chicken. Season to taste with salt and pepper. Bring to a boil, then lower the heat and simmer for 25 minutes, until the chicken and potatoes are tender and cooked through.

3 Stir in the cream and cook for another 2 minutes, then remove from the heat and ladle into serving bowls. Garnish with the cooked bacon and flat-leaf parsley and serve immediately.

chicken & broccoli soup

serves 4-6

- ½ head of broccoli
- 4 tbsp unsalted butter
- 1 onion, chopped
- generous 2 tbsp basmati rice
- 8 oz/225 g skinless, boneless chicken breast, cut into thin slivers
- scant ¼ cup all-purpose whole wheat flour
- 1¼ cups milk
- 2 cups chicken stock
- generous ⅓ cup corn kernels
- salt and pepper

1 Break the broccoli into small florets and cook in a pan of lightly salted boiling water for 3 minutes, drain, then plunge into cold water and set aside.

2 Melt the butter in a pan over medium heat, add the onion, rice, and chicken, and cook for 5 minutes, stirring frequently.

3 Remove the pan from the heat and stir in the flour. Return to the heat and cook for 2 minutes, stirring constantly. Stir in the milk and then the stock. Bring to a boil, stirring constantly, then reduce the heat and let simmer for 10 minutes.

4 Drain the broccoli and add to the pan with the corn and salt and pepper to taste. Let simmer for 5 minutes, or until the rice is tender, then serve immediately.

chicken, mushroom & barley soup

serves 4
- ⅓ cup pearl barley, rinsed and drained
- 2 tbsp butter
- 1 large onion, sliced
- 1 large leek, trimmed and sliced
- 4 cups chicken stock
- 1 lb/450 g skinless, boneless chicken breast, chopped
- 9 oz/250 g cremini mushrooms, sliced
- 1 large carrot, peeled and chopped
- 1 tbsp chopped fresh oregano
- 1 bay leaf
- salt and pepper
- sprigs of fresh flat-leaf parsley, to garnish
- fresh crusty bread, to serve

1 Bring a pan of water to a boil. Add the barley and boil over high heat for 5 minutes, skimming off any foam from the surface when necessary. Remove from the heat and set aside.

2 Melt the butter in a large pan. Add the onion and cook over medium heat, stirring, for 3 minutes, until slightly softened. Add the leek and cook for another 4 minutes, stirring. Stir in the stock, then drain the barley and add to the pan. Season to taste with salt and pepper. Bring to a boil, then lower the heat and simmer for 45 minutes. Add the chicken, mushrooms, carrot, oregano, and bay leaf. Cook for another 30 minutes.

3 Remove from the heat and discard the bay leaf. Ladle into serving bowls, garnish with sprigs of fresh flat-leaf parsley, and serve immediately with fresh crusty bread.

chicken gumbo soup

serves 6

- 2 tbsp olive oil
- 4 tbsp all-purpose flour
- 1 onion, finely chopped
- 1 small green bell pepper, seeded and finely chopped
- 1 celery stalk, finely chopped
- 5 cups chicken stock
- 14 oz/400 g canned chopped tomatoes
- 3 garlic cloves, finely chopped or crushed
- 4½ oz/125 g okra, stems removed, cut into ¼ inch/5-mm thick slices
- 4 tbsp white rice
- 1½ cups cubed, cooked chicken
- 4 oz/115 g cooked garlic sausage, sliced or cubed
- salt and pepper

1 Heat the oil in a large, heavy-bottom saucepan over medium–low heat and stir in the flour. Cook for about 15 minutes, stirring occasionally, until the mixture is a rich golden brown.

2 Add the onion, green bell pepper, and celery and continue cooking for about 10 minutes, until the onion softens.

3 Slowly pour in the stock and bring to a boil, stirring well and scraping the bottom of the pan to mix in the flour. Remove the pan from the heat.

4 Add the tomatoes and garlic. Stir in the okra and rice and season to taste with salt and pepper. Reduce the heat, cover, and simmer for 20 minutes, or until the okra is tender.

5 Add the chicken and sausage and continue simmering for about 10 minutes. Taste and adjust the seasoning, if necessary. Ladle into warmed bowls and serve immediately.

curried chicken soup

serves 4–6

- 4 tbsp butter
- 2 onions, chopped
- 1 small turnip, cut into small dice
- 2 carrots, finely sliced
- 1 apple, peeled, cored, and chopped
- 2 tbsp mild curry powder
- 5 cups chicken stock
- juice of ½ lemon
- 1¼ cups, cubed, cold, cooked chicken
- 2 tbsp chopped fresh cilantro, plus extra to garnish
- salt and pepper
- ½ cup cooked rice, to serve

1 Melt the butter in a large saucepan over medium heat, add the onions, and sauté gently, until soft but not brown.

2 Add the turnip, carrots, and apple and continue to cook for an additional 3–4 minutes.

3 Stir in the curry powder until the vegetables are well coated, then pour in the stock. Bring to a boil, cover, and simmer for about 45 minutes. Season with salt and pepper to taste and add the lemon juice.

4 Transfer the soup to a food processor or blender. Process until smooth and return to the rinsed-out saucepan. Add the chicken and cilantro to the saucepan and heat through.

5 Place a spoonful of rice in each serving bowl and pour the soup over the top. Garnish with cilantro and serve immediately.

chicken, leek & prune soup

serves 4-6
- 2 tbsp butter
- 12 oz/350 g skinless, boneless chicken breast, diced
- 12 oz/350 g leeks, cut into 1-inch/2.5-cm pieces
- 5 cups chicken stock
- 1 bouquet garni (see page 86)
- 8 pitted prunes, halved
- scant 1 cup cooked rice
- 1 red bell pepper, diced (optional)
- salt and white pepper

1 Melt the butter in a large pan. Add the chicken and leeks and cook for 8 minutes.

2 Add the chicken stock and bouquet garni to the pan and stir well, then season to taste with salt and pepper. Bring to a boil and let simmer for 45 minutes.

3 Add the prunes to the pan with the cooked rice and diced bell pepper, if using, and let simmer for 20 minutes.

4 Remove the bouquet garni from the soup and discard. Ladle into warmed soup bowls and serve immediately.

chicken & corn soup

Serves 6
- 1 roasted chicken, about 3 lb/1.3 kg
- ½ tsp saffron threads
- 3 tbsp corn oil
- 2 onions, thinly sliced
- 3 celery stalks, sliced
- 7½ cups vegetable stock
- 8 black peppercorns
- 1 mace blade
- 4 oz/115 g egg noodles
- 2⅓ cups frozen corn
- pinch of dried sage
- 2 tbsp chopped fresh flat-leaf parsley
- salt and pepper

1 Remove the skin from the chicken, cut the meat off the bones, and cut into small pieces. Put the saffron into a bowl, pour in hot water to cover, and let soak.

2 Heat the oil in a pan. Add the onions and celery and cook over low heat, stirring occasionally, for 5 minutes, until softened. Increase the heat to medium, pour in the vegetable stock, add the peppercorns and mace, and bring to a boil. Reduce the heat and simmer for 25 minutes.

3 Increase the heat to medium, add the chicken, noodles, corn, sage, parsley, and saffron with its soaking water, season to taste with salt and pepper, and bring back to a boil. Reduce the heat and simmer for another 20 minutes.

4 Remove the pan from the heat, taste and adjust the seasoning, if necessary, ladle into warmed bowls, and serve immediately.

chicken & almond soup

serves 6

- ½ cup butter
- 2 leeks, chopped
- 1½ tbsp finely chopped fresh ginger
- 6 oz/175 g skinless, boneless chicken breast, diced
- 2 carrots, chopped
- ¾ cup shelled fresh or frozen peas
- 2 green chiles, seeded and chopped
- 1¼ cups ground almonds
- 1 tbsp chopped fresh cilantro, plus extra to garnish
- generous 3 cups vegetable stock
- 1½ cups light cream
- salt and pepper
- grated Parmesan cheese, to serve

1 Melt the butter in a pan. Add the leeks and ginger and cook over low heat, stirring occasionally, for 5 minutes, until softened. Add the chicken, carrots, peas, chiles, and ground almonds and cook, stirring constantly, for 10 minutes.

2 Stir in the cilantro, remove from the heat, and let cool slightly. Spoon the chicken mixture into a food processor and process until very finely chopped. Add the vegetable stock and process until smooth.

3 Return the mixture to the pan, season to taste with salt and pepper, and bring to a boil. Reduce the heat to very low and gradually stir in the cream; do not let the soup boil. Simmer, stirring frequently, for 2 minutes. Ladle into warmed bowls, sprinkle with chopped cilantro and Parmesan and serve immediately.

whole chicken soup

serves 6–8

- 3½ oz/100 g Yunnan ham or ordinary ham, chopped
- 2 dried Chinese mushrooms, soaked in warm water for 20 minutes
- ¾ cup fresh or canned bamboo shoots, rinsed (if using fresh shoots, boil in water first for 30 minutes)
- 1 whole chicken
- 1 tbsp slivered scallion
- 8 slices fresh ginger
- 8 oz/225 g lean pork, chopped
- 2 tsp Chinese rice wine
- 12 cups water
- 2 tsp salt
- 10½ oz/300 g Chinese cabbage, cut into large chunks

sesame and scallion dipping sauce

- 2 tbsp light soy sauce
- ¼ tsp sesame oil
- 2 tbsp finely chopped scallion

1 To make the dipping sauce, combine all the ingredients and set aside.

2 Blanch the Yunnan ham in boiling water for 30 seconds. Skim the surface, then remove the ham and set aside. Squeeze out any excess water from the mushrooms, then finely slice and discard any tough stems. Chop the bamboo shoots into small cubes.

3 Stuff the chicken with the scallion and ginger. Put all the ingredients except the cabbage and dipping sauce in a flameproof casserole. Bring to a boil, then lower the heat and simmer, covered, for 1 hour. Add the cabbage and simmer for an additional 3 minutes.

4 Remove the chicken skin before serving, then place a chunk of chicken meat in individual bowls, adding pieces of vegetable and the other meats, and pour the soup on top. Serve immediately with the sesame and spring onion sauce for dipping the chicken pieces into.

chicken & lentil soup

serves 6

- 3 tbsp olive oil
- 1 large onion, chopped
- 2 leeks, chopped
- 2 carrots, chopped
- 2 celery stalks, chopped
- scant 2½ cups chopped white mushrooms
- 4 tbsp dry white wine
- 5 cups vegetable stock
- 1 bay leaf
- 2 tsp dried mixed herbs
- ¾ cup French green lentils
- scant 2½ cups diced cooked chicken
- salt and pepper

1 Heat the oil in a large pan. Add the onion, leeks, carrots, celery, and mushrooms and cook over low heat, stirring occasionally, for 5–7 minutes, until softened but not colored.

2 Increase the heat to medium, pour in the wine, and cook for 2–3 minutes, until the alcohol has evaporated, then pour in the vegetable stock. Bring to a boil, add the bay leaf and herbs, reduce the heat, cover, and simmer for 30 minutes.

3 Add the lentils, re-cover the pan, and simmer, stirring occasionally for an additional 40 minutes, until they are tender.

4 Stir in the chicken, season to taste with salt and pepper, and simmer for another 5–10 minutes, until heated through. Remove and discard the bay leaf and serve immediately

italian chicken soup

serves 4
- 1 lb/450 g skinless, boneless chicken breasts, cut into thin strips
- 5 cups chicken stock
- ⅔ cup heavy cream
- 4 oz/115 g dried vermicelli
- 1 tbsp cornstarch
- 3 tbsp milk
- 6 oz/175 g canned corn kernels, drained
- salt and pepper

1 Place the chicken in a large pan and pour in the chicken stock and cream. Bring to a boil, then reduce the heat and let simmer for 20 minutes.

2 Meanwhile, bring a large heavy-bottom pan of lightly salted water to a boil. Add the pasta, return to a boil, and cook for 8–10 minutes, or according to the package directions, until just tender but still firm to the bite. Drain the pasta well and keep warm.

3 Season the soup to taste with salt and pepper. Mix the cornstarch and milk together until a smooth paste forms, then stir it into the soup. Add the corn and pasta and heat through. Ladle into warmed serving bowls and serve immediately.

chicken & rice soup

serves 4

- 6¼ cups chicken stock
- 2 small carrots,
  very thinly sliced
- 1 celery stalk, finely diced
- 1 baby leek, halved
  lengthwise and thinly sliced
- ¾ cup young green peas,
  defrosted if frozen
- 1 cup cooked rice
- 1 cup sliced, cooked
  chicken
- 2 tsp chopped fresh
  tarragon
- 1 tbsp chopped fresh
  parsley
- salt and pepper
- sprigs of fresh parsley,
  to garnish

1 Put the stock in a large saucepan and add the carrots, celery, and leek. Bring to a boil, reduce the heat to low, and simmer gently, partially covered, for 10 minutes.

2 Stir in the peas, rice, and chicken and continue cooking for an additional 10–15 minutes, or until the vegetables are tender.

3 Add the chopped tarragon and parsley, then taste and adjust the seasoning, adding salt and pepper, if needed.

4 Ladle the soup into warmed bowls, garnish with parsley, and serve immediately.

chicken soup with rice & leeks

serves 6
- 2 tbsp olive oil
- 3 leeks, chopped
- 6 skinless, boneless chicken thighs, diced
- generous ¼ cup long-grain rice
- 5⅔ cups vegetable stock
- dash of Worcestershire sauce
- 6 fresh chives, chopped
- 6 thin bacon slices
- 2 tbsp chopped fresh flat-leaf parsley
- salt and pepper

1 Heat the oil in a pan. Add the leeks and cook over low heat, stirring occasionally, for 5 minutes, until softened. Add the chicken, increase the heat to medium, and cook, stirring frequently, for 2 minutes. Add the rice and cook, stirring constantly, for an additional 2 minutes.

2 Pour in the vegetable stock, add the Worcestershire sauce and chives, and bring to a boil. Reduce the heat, cover, and simmer for 20–25 minutes.

3 Meanwhile, preheat the broiler. Broil the bacon for 2–4 minutes on each side, until crisp. Remove and let cool, then crumble.

4 Season the soup to taste with salt and pepper and stir in the parsley. Ladle into warmed bowls, sprinkle with the crumbled bacon, and serve immediately.

thai chicken soup

serves 4

- 1 tbsp sesame oil
  or chili oil
- 2 garlic cloves, chopped
- 2 scallions, trimmed
  and sliced
- 1 leek, trimmed and
  finely sliced
- 1 tbsp grated fresh ginger
- 1 red chile, seeded and
  finely chopped
- 12 oz/350 g skinless,
  boneless chicken breast,
  cut into strips
- scant 3½ cups
  chicken stock
- 2 tbsp rice wine
- 1 tbsp chopped lemongrass
- 6 kaffir lime leaves,
  finely shredded
- 7 oz/200 g fine egg noodles
- salt and pepper

1 Heat the oil in a wok or large pan. Add the garlic and cook over medium heat, stirring, for 1 minute, then add the scallions, leek, ginger, and chile and cook, stirring, for another 3 minutes. Add the chicken, stock, and rice wine, bring to a boil, and simmer for 20 minutes. Stir in the lemongrass and lime leaves.

2 Bring a separate pan of water to a boil and add the noodles. Cook for 3 minutes, or according to the package directions, drain well, then add them to the soup. Season to taste with salt and pepper. Cook for an additional 2 minutes. Remove from the heat, ladle into warmed serving bowls, and serve immediately.

chicken noodle soup

serves 4–6

- 2 skinless, boneless chicken breasts
- 5 cups water or chicken stock
- 3 carrots, peeled and cut into ¼-inch/5-mm slices
- 3 oz/85 g vermicelli (or other small noodles)
- salt and pepper
- fresh tarragon leaves, to garnish

1 Place the chicken breasts in a large saucepan, add the water, and bring to a simmer. Cook for 25–30 minutes. Skim any foam from the surface, if necessary. Remove the chicken from the stock and keep warm.

2 Continue to simmer the stock, add the carrots and vermicelli, and cook for 4–5 minutes.

3 Thinly slice or shred the chicken breasts and place in warmed serving dishes.

4 Season the soup to taste with salt and pepper and pour over the chicken. Serve immediately garnished with the tarragon.

thai chicken-coconut soup

serves 4
- 4 oz/115 g dried cellophane noodles
- 5 cups chicken or vegetable stock
- 1 lemongrass stalk, crushed
- ½-inch/1-cm piece fresh ginger, peeled and very finely chopped
- 2 fresh kaffir lime leaves, thinly sliced
- 1 fresh red chile, or to taste, seeded and thinly sliced
- 2 skinless, boneless chicken breasts, thinly sliced
- scant 1 cup coconut cream
- 2 tbsp nam pla (fish sauce)
- 1 tbsp fresh lime juice
- scant ½ cup bean sprouts
- 4 scallions, green part only, finely sliced
- fresh cilantro leaves, to garnish

1 Soak the dried noodles in a large bowl with enough lukewarm water to cover for 20 minutes, until soft. Alternatively, cook according to the package instructions. Drain well and set aside.

2 Meanwhile, bring the stock to a boil in a large pan over high heat. Lower the heat, add the lemongrass, ginger, lime leaves, and chile and simmer for 5 minutes. Add the chicken and continue simmering for an additional 3 minutes, or until cooked. Stir in the coconut cream, nam pla, and lime juice and continue simmering for 3 minutes. Add the bean sprouts and scallions and simmer for an additional 1 minute. Taste and gradually add extra nam pla or lime juice at this point, if needed. Remove and discard the lemongrass stalk.

3 Divide the noodles among 4 bowls. Bring the soup back to a boil, then ladle into the bowls. The heat of the soup will warm the noodles. To garnish, sprinkle with cilantro leaves. Serve immediately.

oriental chicken balls & greens in broth

serves 6
- 8 cups chicken stock
- 3 oz/85 g shiitake mushrooms, thinly sliced
- 6 oz/175 g bok choy or other Asian greens, sliced into thin ribbons
- 6 scallions, finely sliced
- salt and pepper

chicken balls
- 1 oz/25 g ground chicken
- ½ cup finely chopped, fresh spinach
- 2 scallions, finely chopped
- 1 garlic clove, very finely chopped
- pinch of Chinese 5-spice powder
- 1 tsp soy sauce

1 To make the chicken balls, put the chicken, spinach, scallions, and garlic in a bowl. Add the 5-spice powder and soy sauce and mix until combined.

2 Shape the chicken mixture into 24 balls. Place them in one layer in a steamer that will fit over the top of a saucepan.

3 Bring the stock just to a boil in a saucepan that will accommodate the steamer. Regulate the heat so that the liquid bubbles gently. Add the mushrooms to the stock and place the steamer, covered, on top of the pan. Steam for 10 minutes. Remove the steamer and set aside on a plate.

4 Add the bok choy and scallions to the pan and cook gently in the stock for 3–4 minutes, or until the leaves are wilted. Taste the soup and adjust the seasoning, if necessary.

5 Divide the chicken balls evenly among warmed bowls and ladle the soup over them. Serve immediately.

chicken soup with ginger & coconut milk

serves 6

- 14 oz/400g skinless, boneless chicken breast, cut into strips
- ½ cup Thai fragrant rice
- 1 lemongrass stalk, bruised
- 4 garlic cloves, coarsely chopped
- 2 green chiles, seeded and sliced
- 4 kaffir lime leaves, torn
- 1-inch/2.5-cm piece fresh ginger, chopped
- 4 tbsp chopped fresh cilantro, plus extra to garnish
- 6¾ cups vegetable stock
- 1¾ cups canned coconut milk
- 4 scallions, thinly sliced
- 1 cup baby corn cobs
- 4 oz/115 g white mushrooms, halved
- salt
- chopped red chile, to garnish

1 Put the chicken, rice, lemongrass, garlic, chiles, lime leaves, ginger, and cilantro into a pan, pour in the vegetable stock and coconut milk, and bring to a boil over medium heat, stirring occasionally. Reduce the heat, cover, and simmer for 1 hour.

2 Remove the pan from the heat and let cool slightly. Remove and discard the lemongrass and kaffir lime leaves. Ladle the soup into a food processor or blender, and process until smooth.

3 Return the soup to the rinsed-out pan, season to taste with salt, and add the scallions, corn cobs, and mushrooms. Bring back to a boil, then reduce the heat and simmer for 5 minutes.

4 Remove the pan from the heat. Ladle the soup into warmed bowls, garnish with chopped cilantro and chile, and serve immediately.

turkey soup with rice, mushrooms & sage

serves 4

- 3 tbsp butter
- 1 onion, finely chopped
- 1 celery stalk, finely chopped
- 25 large fresh sage leaves, finely chopped
- 4 tbsp all-purpose flour
- 5 cups turkey or chicken stock
- ⅔ cup brown rice
- 9 oz/250 g mushrooms, sliced
- 1½ cups diced, cooked turkey
- ¾ cup heavy cream
- salt and pepper
- sprigs of fresh sage, to garnish
- freshly grated Parmesan cheese, to serve

1 Melt half the butter in a large saucepan over medium–low heat. Add the onion, celery, and sage and cook for 3–4 minutes, until the onion is softened, stirring frequently. Stir in the flour and continue cooking for 2 minutes.

2 Slowly add about one-quarter of the stock and stir well. Pour in the remaining stock, and bring just to a boil.

3 Stir in the rice and season to taste with salt and pepper. Reduce the heat and simmer gently, partially covered, for about 30 minutes until the rice is just tender, stirring occasionally.

4 Meanwhile, melt the remaining butter in a large skillet over medium heat. Add the mushrooms and season to taste with salt and pepper. Cook for about 8 minutes, until they are golden brown.

5 Add the turkey and mushrooms to the soup and stir in the cream. Continue simmering for about 10 minutes, until heated through. Ladle into warmed bowls, garnish with sage, and serve immediately with Parmesan cheese.

lemon turkey soup with mushrooms

serves 4

- 12 oz/350 g boneless turkey, cut into ½-inch/1-cm pieces
- 4 cups chicken stock
- 1 onion, quartered
- 2 carrots, thinly sliced
- 2 garlic cloves, halved
- 1 pared strip lemon rind
- 1 bay leaf
- 1 tbsp butter
- 12 oz/350 g small button mushrooms, quartered
- 4 tbsp cornstarch
- ½ cup heavy cream
- freshly grated nutmeg
- fresh lemon juice, to taste (optional)
- 1–2 tbsp chopped fresh parsley
- salt and pepper

1 Put the turkey in a large saucepan and add the stock. Bring just to a boil and skim off any foam that rises to the surface. Add the onion, carrots, garlic, lemon rind, and bay leaf. Season to taste with salt and pepper. Reduce the heat and simmer, partially covered, for about 45 minutes, stirring occasionally, until the turkey is cooked.

2 Remove the turkey and carrots with a slotted spoon and reserve, covered. Strain the stock into a clean saucepan. Discard the onion, garlic, lemon rind, and bay leaf.

3 Melt the butter in a skillet over medium-high heat. Add the mushrooms, season, and cook gently until lightly golden. Reserve with the turkey and carrots.

4 Mix together the cornstarch and cream. Bring the cooking liquid just to a boil and whisk in the cream mixture. Boil very gently for 2–3 minutes until it thickens, whisking almost constantly.

5 Add the reserved meat and vegetables to the soup and simmer over low heat for about 5 minutes until heated through. Taste and adjust the seasoning, adding nutmeg and a squeeze of lemon juice, if using. Stir in the parsley, then ladle into warmed bowls and serve immediately.

turkey, leek & blue cheese soup

serves 4
- 4 tbsp butter
- 1 large onion, chopped
- 1 leek, trimmed and sliced
- 2⅓ cups sliced, cooked turkey
- 2½ cups chicken stock
- 5½ oz/150 g blue cheese
- ⅔ cup heavy cream
- 1 tbsp chopped fresh tarragon
- pepper
- fresh tarragon leaves and croutons (see page 9), to garnish

1 Melt the butter in a pan over medium heat. Add the onion and cook, stirring, for 4 minutes, until slightly softened. Add the leek and cook for another 3 minutes.

2 Add the turkey to the pan and pour in the stock. Bring to a boil, then reduce the heat and simmer gently, stirring occasionally, for about 15 minutes. Remove from the heat and let cool a little.

3 Transfer half of the soup into a food processor and blend until smooth. Return the mixture to the pan with the rest of the soup, stir in the blue cheese, cream, and tarragon and season to taste with pepper. Reheat gently, stirring. Remove from the heat, ladle into warmed soup bowls, garnish with tarragon and croutons and serve immediately.

turkey & lentil soup

serves 4
- 1 tbsp olive oil
- 1 garlic clove, chopped
- 1 large onion, chopped
- 3 cups sliced white mushrooms
- 1 red bell pepper, seeded and chopped
- 6 tomatoes, skinned, seeded, and chopped
- 4 cups chicken stock
- ⅔ cup red wine
- ⅔ cup cauliflower florets
- 1 carrot, chopped
- 1 cup red lentils
- 2½ cups chopped, cooked turkey
- 1 zucchini, chopped
- 1 tbsp shredded fresh basil, plus extra sprigs to garnish
- salt and pepper

1 Heat the oil in a large pan. Add the garlic and onion and cook over medium heat, stirring, for 3 minutes, until slightly softened. Add the mushrooms, bell pepper, and tomatoes, and cook for another 5 minutes, stirring. Pour in the stock and red wine, then add the cauliflower, carrot, and red lentils. Season to taste with salt and pepper. Bring to a boil, then lower the heat and simmer for 25 minutes, until the vegetables are tender and cooked through.

2 Add the turkey and zucchini to the pan and cook for 10 minutes. Stir in the shredded basil and cook for another 5 minutes, then remove from the heat and ladle into serving bowls. Garnish with fresh basil and serve immediately.

oriental duck broth

serves 4–6

- 2 duck leg quarters, skinned
- 4 cups water
- 2½ cups chicken stock
- 1-inch/2.5-cm piece fresh ginger
- 1 large carrot, sliced
- 1 onion, sliced
- 1 leek, sliced
- 3 garlic cloves, crushed
- 1 tsp black peppercorns
- 2 tbsp soy sauce, or to taste
- 1 small carrot, cut into thin strips or slivers
- 1 small leek, cut into thin strips or slivers
- 3½ oz/100 g shiitake mushrooms, thinly sliced
- 1 oz/25 g watercress leaves
- salt and pepper

1 Put the duck in a large saucepan with the water. Bring just to a boil and skim off the foam that rises to the surface. Add the stock, ginger, carrot, onion, leek, garlic, peppercorns, and soy sauce. Reduce the heat and simmer, partially covered, for 1½ hours.

2 Remove the duck from the stock and set aside. When the duck is cool enough to handle, remove the meat from the bones and slice thinly or shred into bite-size pieces, discarding any fat.

3 Strain the stock and press the vegetables with the back of a spoon to extract all the liquid. Remove as much fat as possible. Discard the vegetables and herbs.

4 Bring the stock just to a boil in a clean saucepan and add the strips of carrot and leek, the mushrooms, and duck meat. Reduce the heat and cook gently for 5 minutes, or until the carrot is just tender.

5 Stir in the watercress and continue simmering for 1–2 minutes, until it is wilted. Taste the soup and adjust the seasoning, if needed, adding a little more soy sauce, if desired. Ladle the soup into warmed bowls and serve immediately.

duck with scallion soup

serves 4

- 2 duck breasts, skin on
- 2 tbsp red curry paste
- 2 tbsp vegetable or peanut oil
- bunch of scallions, chopped
- 2 garlic cloves, crushed
- 2-inch/5-cm piece fresh ginger, grated
- 2 carrots, thinly sliced
- 1 red bell pepper, seeded and cut into strips
- 4 cups chicken stock
- 2 tbsp sweet chili sauce
- 3–4 tbsp Thai soy sauce
- 14 oz/400 g canned straw mushrooms, drained

1 Slash the skin of the duck 3 or 4 times with a sharp knife and rub in the curry paste. Cook the duck breasts, skin-side down, in a wok or skillet over high heat for 2–3 minutes. Turn over, reduce the heat, and cook for an additional 3–4 minutes, until cooked through. Lift out and slice thickly. Set aside and keep warm.

2 Meanwhile, heat the oil in a wok or large skillet and stir-fry half the scallions, the garlic, ginger, carrots, and red bell pepper for 2–3 minutes. Pour in the stock and add the chili sauce, soy sauce, and mushrooms. Bring to a boil, reduce the heat, and simmer for 4–5 minutes.

3 Ladle the soup into warmed bowls, top with the duck slices, and garnish with the remaining scallions. Serve immediately.

Mmmm...
fish & seafood

fisherman's soup

serves 6

- 2 lb/900 g fillets of mixed white fish and shellfish, such as cod, flounder, halibut, monkfish, sea bass, whiting, and peeled shrimp
- ⅔ cup olive oil
- 2 large onions, sliced
- 2 celery stalks, thinly sliced
- 2 garlic cloves, chopped
- ⅔ cup white wine
- 4 canned tomatoes, chopped
- pared rind of 1 orange
- 1 tsp chopped fresh thyme
- 2 tbsp chopped fresh parsley
- 2 bay leaves
- salt and pepper
- croutons (see page 9) and sprigs of fresh thyme, to garnish
- lemon wedges, to serve

1 Cut the fish into fairly large, thick, serving portions, discarding any skin.

2 Heat the oil in a large pan, add the onion, celery, and garlic and fry for 5 minutes, until softened.

3 Add the fish and shrimp to the pan then add the wine, tomatoes, orange rind, thyme, parsley, bay leaves, salt and pepper to taste, and enough cold water to cover. Bring to a boil, then simmer, uncovered, for 15 minutes.

4 Garnish the soup with croutons and thyme, and serve immediately with lemon wedges.

fish & sweet potato soup

serves 6

- 12 oz/350 g white fish fillet, skinned
- scant 1 cup diced sweet potato
- 1 onion, chopped
- 2 carrots, diced
- ½ tsp ground cinnamon
- 7½ cups vegetable stock
- 14 oz/400 g clams
- ⅔ cup dry white wine
- 1 cup light cream
- salt and pepper
- extra virgin olive oil, for drizzling
- chopped fresh flat-leaf parsley, to garnish

1 Put the fish, sweet potato, onion, carrots, and cinnamon into a pan, pour in 4 cups of the vegetable stock, and bring to a boil. Reduce the heat, cover, and simmer for 30 minutes.

2 Meanwhile, scrub the clams under cold running water and remove any with broken shells or that do not shut immediately when sharply tapped. Put them into a pan, pour in the wine, cover, and cook over high heat, shaking the pan occasionally, for 3–5 minutes, until the clams have opened. Remove from the heat and lift out the clams with a slotted spoon, reserving the cooking liquid. Discard any clams that remain shut. Strain the cooking liquid through a cheesecloth-lined strainer into a bowl.

3 Remove the pan of fish and vegetables from the heat and let cool slightly, then ladle the mixture into a food processor or blender, and process until smooth.

4 Return the soup to the pan, add the remaining stock and the reserved cooking liquid, and bring back to a boil. Reduce the heat and gradually stir in the cream; do not let the soup boil. Add the clams, season to taste with salt and pepper, and simmer, stirring frequently, for 2 minutes. Drizzle with olive oil, garnish with parsley, and serve immediately.

fish soup with cider

serves 4

- 2 tsp butter
- 1 large leek, thinly sliced
- 2 shallots, finely chopped
- ½ cup hard cider
- 1¼ cups fish stock
- 1⅔ cups diced potatoes
- 1 bay leaf
- 4 tbsp all-purpose flour
- ¾ cup milk
- ¾ cup heavy cream
- 1¾ cups finely chopped, fresh sorrel
- 12 oz/350 g skinless monkfish or cod fillet, cut into 1-inch/2.5-cm pieces
- salt

1 Melt the butter in a large saucepan over medium–low heat. Add the leek and shallots and cook for about 5 minutes, stirring frequently, until they start to soften. Add the cider and bring to a boil.

2 Stir in the stock, potatoes, and bay leaf with a large pinch of salt (unless stock is salty) and bring back to a boil. Reduce the heat, cover, and cook gently for 10 minutes.

3 Put the flour in a small bowl and very slowly whisk in a few tablespoons of the milk to make a thick paste. Stir in a little more to make a smooth liquid.

4 Adjust the heat so the soup bubbles gently. Stir in the flour mixture and cook, stirring frequently, for 5 minutes. Add the remaining milk and half the cream. Continue cooking for about 10 minutes, until the potatoes are tender.

5 Add the sorrel and combine with the remaining cream. Stir the sorrel cream into the soup and add the fish. Continue cooking, stirring occasionally, for about 3 minutes, until the monkfish stiffens or the cod just begins to flake. Taste the soup and adjust the seasoning, if needed. Remove and discard the bay leaf, ladle into warmed bowls, and serve immediately.

mixed fish soup

serves 4
- 1 tbsp butter
- 2 shallots, chopped
- 1 leek, trimmed and sliced
- 3 tbsp all-purpose flour
- generous 2 cups fish stock
- 1 bay leaf
- generous 2 cups milk
- 2 tbsp dry sherry
- 2 tbsp lemon juice
- 10½ oz/300 g white fish fillets, skinned
- 10½ oz/300 g cod fillets, skinned
- 7 oz/200 g canned or freshly cooked crabmeat
- 5½ oz/150 g canned corn kernels, drained
- generous ¾ cup heavy cream
- salt and pepper
- sprigs of fresh dill and wedges of lemon, to garnish

1 Melt the butter in a large pan over medium heat. Add the shallots and leek and cook, stirring, for about 3 minutes, until slightly softened. In a bowl, mix the flour with enough stock to make a smooth paste, then stir it into the pan. Cook, stirring, for 2 minutes, then gradually stir in the remaining stock. Add the bay leaf and season to taste with salt and pepper. Bring to a boil, then lower the heat. Pour in the milk and sherry and stir in the lemon juice. Simmer for 15 minutes.

2 Rinse the white fish and cod under cold running water, then drain and cut into bite-size chunks. Add to the soup with the crabmeat and corn. Cook for 15 minutes, until the fish is tender and cooked through. Stir in the cream. Cook for an additional 2–3 minutes, then remove from the heat and discard the bay leaf.

3 Ladle into serving bowls, garnish with sprigs of fresh dill and lemon wedges, and serve immediately.

miso fish soup

serves 4

- 3½ cups fish or vegetable stock
- 1-inch/2.5-cm piece fresh ginger, grated
- 1 tbsp mirin or dry sherry
- 1 fresh Thai chile, seeded and finely sliced
- ⅔ cup thinly sliced carrots
- 2 oz/55 g daikon, peeled and cut into thin strips or ½ bunch radishes, trimmed and sliced
- 1 yellow bell pepper, seeded and cut into thin strips
- 3 oz/85 g shiitake mushrooms, sliced if large
- 1½ oz/40 g fine egg noodles
- 8 oz/225 g sole fillets, skinned and cut into strips
- 1 tbsp miso paste
- 4 scallions, trimmed and shredded

1 Pour the stock into a large saucepan and add the ginger, mirin, and chile. Bring to a boil then reduce the heat, and simmer for 5 minutes.

2 Add the carrot with the daikon, bell pepper strips, mushrooms, and noodles and simmer for an additional 3 minutes.

3 Add the fish strips with the miso paste and continue to cook for 2 minutes, or until the fish is tender. Divide equally between 4 serving bowls, top with the scallions, and serve immediately.

fish soup with semolina & dill dumplings

serves 6

- ¾ cup diced chorizo
- 1 lb 2 oz/500 g white fish fillets, skinned and diced
- 1 tbsp sweet paprika
- pinch of cayenne pepper
- 6¼ cups vegetable stock
- 4 potatoes, diced
- 4 tomatoes, peeled and diced
- 1 tbsp chopped fresh flat-leaf parsley
- salt and pepper

semolina dumplings

- ½ cup fine semolina
- pinch of salt
- 1 tbsp chopped fresh dill
- 1 egg
- 3 tbsp milk

1 Put the chorizo into a heavy pan and cook over medium–low heat, stirring frequently, for 5 minutes, until lightly browned. Add the fish and cook, occasionally stirring gently, for 2 minutes.

2 Sprinkle in the paprika and cayenne, pour in the vegetable stock, and bring to a boil. Reduce the heat, cover, and simmer for 10 minutes.

3 Add the potatoes, tomatoes, and parsley, stir gently, re-cover the pan, and simmer for 10 minutes.

4 Meanwhile, make the semolina and dill dumplings. Combine the semolina, salt, and dill in a bowl. Lightly beat together the egg and milk in another bowl, then stir into the dry ingredients until thoroughly combined. Cover and let rest in the refrigerator for 10 minutes.

5 Scoop up tablespoonfuls of the dumpling mixture and add them to the soup. Season to taste with salt and pepper. Re-cover the pan and simmer for another 10 minutes. Serve immediately.

genoese fish soup

serves 4

- 2 tbsp butter
- 1 onion, chopped
- 1 garlic clove,
  finely chopped
- 2 oz/55 g rindless bacon,
  diced
- 2 celery stalks, chopped
- 14 oz/400 g canned
  chopped tomatoes
- ⅔ cup dry white wine
- 1¼ cups fish stock
- 4 fresh basil leaves, torn
- 2 tbsp chopped fresh
  flat-leaf parsley,
  plus extra to garnish
- 1 lb/450 g white fish fillets,
  such as cod or monkfish,
  skinned and cut into
  bite-size pieces
- 4 oz/115 g cooked,
  peeled shrimp
- salt and pepper

1 Melt the butter in a large, heavy-bottom saucepan. Add the onion and garlic and cook over low heat, stirring occasionally, for 5 minutes, or until softened.

2 Add the bacon and celery and cook, stirring frequently, for an additional 2 minutes.

3 Add the tomatoes, wine, stock, basil, and the parsley. Season to taste with salt and pepper. Bring to a boil, then reduce the heat and simmer for 10 minutes.

4 Add the fish and cook for 5 minutes, or until it is opaque. Add the shrimp and heat through gently for 3 minutes. Ladle into warmed serving bowls, garnish with the chopped parsley, and serve immediately.

spicy & sour fish & pineapple soup

serves 6
- 1 lb/450 g skinless, boneless catfish or cod fillets, cut into large chunks
- ⅓ cup tamarind concentrate
- 1⅓ cups bite-size pineapple chunks
- 1 large ripe tomato, peeled, halved, seeded, and cut into 8 wedges
- 2 or more red Thai chiles, seeded and thinly sliced into rounds
- 1 tbsp nam pla (fish sauce)
- 12 fresh Thai basil leaves, freshly torn
- 6 fresh saw leaves, freshly torn, or ⅓ cup fresh cilantro leaves
- salt and pepper
- garlic oil, to garnish

light fish stock
- 12 cups water
- 2½ lb/1.1 kg fish heads and bones
- ¾-inch/2-cm piece fresh ginger, peeled and thinly sliced
- 4 scallions, trimmed and crushed
- 2 to 3 tbsp nam pla (fish sauce)

1 For the stock, put the water, fish heads and bones in a large saucepan and bring to a boil over high heat. Reduce the heat to medium–low, then add the ginger, scallions, and nam pla, and simmer for 1½ hours, or until reduced by about half, skimming off any foam. Strain the stock, discarding the solids, and remove any fat.

2 Season the fish with salt and pepper to taste. Cover with plastic wrap and refrigerate for up to 30 minutes.

3 Pour the stock into a medium saucepan and bring to a gentle boil over medium heat. Reduce the heat to medium–low, then add the tamarind concentrate, pineapple, tomato, chiles, and nam pla and cook for 10 minutes. Add the fish chunks and cook for 5 minutes, or until opaque and fork-tender.

4 Ladle the soup into small individual bowls. Scatter over the torn basil and saw leaves and drizzle with garlic oil to garnish. Serve immediately.

thai tom yum soup with fish

serves 6

- 5½ cups light chicken stock
- 6 lemongrass stalks, crushed to release their flavor
- 3 tbsp very finely chopped cilantro roots
- 10 kaffir lime leaves, central stalks torn off
- 1 red chile, seeded and finely chopped
- 1-inch/2.5-cm piece of galangal (or fresh ginger), peeled and thinly sliced
- 3 tbsp nam pla (fish sauce)
- 1 tbsp sugar
- 1 lb 2 oz/500 g shrimp, peeled (except for the tails) and deveined
- 1 lb 2 oz/500 g firm white fish, such as cod or monkfish, chopped into bite-size pieces
- 8 oz/225 g canned bamboo shoots or water chestnuts
- 12 cherry tomatoes, halved
- juice of 2 limes
- handful of fresh cilantro leaves and handful of fresh basil leaves, chopped, to garnish

1 Pour the stock into a large saucepan and add the lemongrass, cilantro roots, lime leaves, chile, galangal, nam pla, and sugar. Cover the saucepan. Bring to a boil, then reduce the heat and simmer for 10 minutes.

2 Add the shrimp, fish, and bamboo shoots and simmer for an additional 4 minutes. Add the tomatoes and lime juice and check the seasoning, adding more nam pla and sugar, if necessary.

3 Remove and discard the lemongrass stalks, then ladle the soup into warmed bowls and scatter over the cilantro and basil leaves. Serve immediately.

thai salmon laksa

serves 4
- juice and zest of 2 limes
- 2 tbsp sunflower oil
- 1 red chile, seeded and finely chopped
- 4 garlic cloves, peeled and crushed
- 1-inch/2.5-cm piece fresh ginger, peeled and grated
- 1 tsp ground coriander
- small bunch of fresh cilantro, plus extra to garnish
- 3 tbsp nam pla (fish sauce)
- 2 cups vegetable or fish stock
- 3½ cups canned coconut milk
- 3 carrots, peeled and thinly sliced
- 14 oz/400 g noodles
- 1 tbsp sesame oil
- 1 tbsp vegetable oil
- 2¾ cups broccoli florets
- 1 lb 2 oz/500 g salmon fillet, skinned, boned, and cut into slices half the width of a finger

1 Put the first 8 ingredients in a food processor or blender and blend to a paste.

2 Place a large saucepan over medium heat and add the paste. Fry for 1 minute.

3 Add the stock, coconut milk, and carrots and bring to a boil. Simmer while you cook the noodles according to the package directions.

4 Drain the noodles and return to the warm saucepan with a splash of sesame oil and vegetable oil. Cover.

5 Add the broccoli to the liquid, bring back to a boil, and then turn off the heat and add the salmon slices, gently stirring them in. Let stand for 3 minutes.

6 Place a handful of noodles in each bowl, then ladle in the laksa. Sprinkle with cilantro leaves and serve immediately.

tuna chowder

serves 4

- 2 tbsp butter
- 1 large garlic clove, chopped
- 1 large onion, sliced
- 1 carrot, peeled and chopped
- 2½ cups fish stock
- 2⅔ cups bite-size potato chunks
- 14 oz/400 g canned chopped tomatoes
- 14 oz/400 g canned cannellini beans, drained
- 1 tbsp tomato paste
- 1 zucchini, trimmed and chopped
- 8 oz/225 g canned tuna, drained
- 1 tbsp chopped fresh basil
- 1 tbsp chopped fresh parsley
- scant ½ cup heavy cream
- salt and pepper
- sprigs of fresh basil, to garnish

1 Melt the butter in a large pan over low heat. Add the garlic and onion and cook, stirring, for 3 minutes, until slightly softened. Add the carrot and cook for another 5 minutes, stirring. Pour in the stock, then add the potatoes, tomatoes, beans, and tomato paste. Season to taste with salt and pepper. Bring to a boil, then reduce the heat, cover the pan, and simmer for 20 minutes.

2 Add the zucchini, tuna, and chopped basil and parsley and cook for an additional 15 minutes. Stir in the cream and cook the soup very gently for another 2 minutes.

3 Remove from the heat and ladle into serving bowls. Garnish with sprigs of fresh basil, and serve immediately.

white fish & shrimp chowder

serves 4

- 1 tbsp butter
- 1 onion, chopped
- 3 tbsp all-purpose flour
- generous 2 cups fish stock
- 1 bay leaf
- generous 2 cups milk
- 2 tbsp dry white wine
- juice and grated rind of 1 lemon
- 1 lb/450 g white fish fillets, skinned
- ¾ cup frozen corn kernels, thawed
- 9 oz/250 g shrimp, cooked and peeled
- generous ¾ cup heavy cream
- salt and pepper
- whole cooked shrimp, to garnish
- fresh green salad, to serve

1 Melt the butter in a large pan over medium heat. Add the onion and cook, stirring, for about 3 minutes, until slightly softened. In a bowl, mix the flour with enough stock to make a smooth paste and stir it into the pan. Cook, stirring, for 2 minutes, then gradually stir in the remaining stock. Add the bay leaf and season to taste with salt and pepper. Bring to a boil, then lower the heat. Pour in the milk and wine, and stir in the lemon juice and grated rind. Simmer for 15 minutes.

2 Rinse the white fish under cold running water, then drain and cut into bite-size chunks. Add them to the soup with the corn. Cook for 15 minutes, until the fish is tender and cooked through. Stir in the shrimp and the cream. Cook for another 2–3 minutes, then remove from the heat and discard the bay leaf.

3 Ladle into serving bowls, garnish with whole cooked shrimp, and serve immediately with a fresh green salad.

199

bouillabaisse

serves 8

- 2 lb 4 oz/1 kg selection of at least 4 different firm white fish fillets, such as red snapper, sea bass, eel, or monkfish, scaled and cleaned, but not skinned
- generous ⅓ cup olive oil
- 2 onions, finely chopped
- 1 fennel bulb, finely chopped
- 4 garlic cloves, crushed
- 2 lb 6 oz/1.2 kg canned chopped plum tomatoes
- 6 cups fish stock
- pinch saffron strands
- grated zest of 1 orange
- bouquet garni (see page 86)
- 1 lb 2 oz/500 g mussels, cleaned
- 1 lb 2 oz/500 g cooked shrimp, shell on
- salt and pepper
- crusty baguette and rouille, to serve

1 Carefully remove the pin bones from the fish, then cut the fillets into bite-size pieces.

2 Heat the oil in a large skillet or wide pan with a lid and gently fry the onion and fennel for about 15 minutes, until softened. Add the garlic and fry for 2 minutes, then add the tomatoes and simmer for 2 minutes. Add the stock, saffron, orange zest, and bouquet garni and bring to a boil. Simmer, uncovered, for 15 minutes.

3 Add the fish pieces, mussels, and shrimp and cover the skillet. Simmer for an additional 5–10 minutes, until the mussels have opened. Discard any that remain closed. Taste and adjust the seasoning, if necessary.

4 Serve hot, with some crusty baguette and rouille.

smoked cod chowder

serves 4

- 2 tbsp butter
- 1 onion, finely chopped
- 1 small celery stalk, finely diced
- 2 potatoes, diced
- 1 carrot, diced
- 1¼ cups boiling water
- 12 oz/350 g smoked cod fillets, skinned and cut into bite-size pieces
- 1¼ cups milk
- salt and pepper
- fresh flat-leaf parsley sprigs, to garnish

1 Melt the butter in a large pan over low heat, add the onion and celery, and cook, stirring frequently, for 5 minutes, or until softened but not browned.

2 Add the potatoes, carrot, water, and salt and pepper to taste. Bring to a boil, then reduce the heat and let simmer for 10 minutes, or until the vegetables are tender. Add the fish to the chowder and cook for an additional 10 minutes.

3 Pour in the milk and heat gently. Taste and adjust the seasoning, if necessary. Serve immediately, garnished with parsley sprigs.

clam chowder

serves 4
- 2 lb/900 g clams
- 4 bacon strips, chopped
- 2 tbsp butter
- 1 onion, chopped
- 1 tbsp chopped fresh thyme
- 1 large potato, diced
- 1¼ cups milk
- 1 bay leaf
- 1⅔ cups heavy cream
- 1 tbsp chopped fresh parsley
- salt and pepper

1 Scrub the clams and put them into a large pan with a splash of water. Cook over high heat for 3–4 minutes, until they open. Discard any that remain closed. Strain the cooking liquid through a cheesecloth-lined strainer into a bowl and reserve. Set aside until cool enough to handle, reserving 8 of the clams for a garnish.

2 Remove the clams from their shells, chopping them roughly if large, and set aside.

3 In a clean pan, fry the bacon until browned and crisp. Drain on paper towels. Add the butter to the same pan, and when it has melted, add the onion. Pan-fry for 4–5 minutes, until soft but not colored. Add the thyme and cook briefly before adding the diced potato, reserved clam cooking liquid, milk, and bay leaf. Bring to a boil and simmer for 10 minutes, or until the potato is just tender.

4 Discard the bay leaf, then transfer to a food processor and blend until smooth, or push through a strainer into a bowl.

5 Add the clams, bacon, and cream. Simmer for another 2–3 minutes, until heated through. Season to taste with salt and pepper. Stir in the chopped parsley and serve, garnished with the reserved clams in their shells.

quick scallop soup with pasta

serves 6
- 1 lb 2 oz/500 g shelled sea scallops
- 1½ cups milk
- generous 6¾ cups vegetable stock
- generous 1 cup frozen baby peas
- 6 oz/175 g taglialini
- 5 tbsp butter
- 2 scallions, finely chopped
- ¾ cup dry white wine
- 3 slices of prosciutto, cut into thin strips
- salt and pepper
- chopped fresh flat-leaf parsley, to garnish

1 Slice the sea scallops in half horizontally and season to taste with salt and pepper.

2 Pour the milk and vegetable stock into a pan, add a pinch of salt, and bring to a boil. Add the peas and pasta, bring back to a boil, and cook for 8–10 minutes, until the taglialini is tender but still firm to the bite.

3 Meanwhile, melt the butter in a skillet. Add the scallions and cook over low heat, stirring occasionally, for 3 minutes. Add the sea scallops and cook for 45 seconds on each side. Pour in the wine, add the prosciutto, and cook for 2–3 minutes.

4 Stir the sea scallop mixture into the soup, taste, and adjust the seasoning, if necessary, and garnish with the parsley. Serve immediately.

crab & vegetable soup

serves 4
- 2 tbsp chili oil
- 1 garlic clove, chopped
- 4 scallions, trimmed and sliced
- 2 red bell peppers, seeded and chopped
- 1 tbsp grated fresh ginger
- 4 cups fish stock
- scant ½ cup coconut milk
- scant ½ cup rice wine or sherry
- 2 tbsp lime juice
- 1 tbsp grated lime zest
- 6 kaffir lime leaves, finely shredded
- 10½ oz/300 g freshly cooked crabmeat
- 7 oz/200 g freshly cooked crab claws
- 5½ oz/150 g canned corn kernels, drained
- 1 tbsp of chopped cilantro, plus a few sprigs to garnish
- salt and pepper

1 Heat the oil in a large pan over medium heat. Add the garlic and scallions and cook, stirring, for about 3 minutes, until slightly softened. Add the bell peppers and ginger and cook for another 4 minutes, stirring. Pour in the stock and season to taste with salt and pepper. Bring to a boil, then lower the heat. Pour in the coconut milk, rice wine, and lime juice and stir in the grated lime zest and kaffir lime leaves. Simmer for 15 minutes.

2 Add the crabmeat and crab claws to the soup with the corn and cilantro. Cook the soup for 15 minutes, until the crabmeat is tender and cooked right through.

3 Remove from the heat and ladle into serving bowls. Garnish with fresh cilantro and serve.

asparagus & crab soup

serves 6

- 2 to 3 cups cooked fresh crabmeat
- 2 cups ¾-inch/2-cm white or green asparagus pieces
- 2 large egg whites, lightly beaten
- 1 tbsp cornstarch
- 2 tbsp water
- salt and pepper
- ½ cup fresh cilantro leaves, for garnishing

chicken or crab stock

- 12 cups water
- 2 lb/900 g meaty chicken bones or crab shells
- ¾-inch/2-cm piece of fresh ginger, peeled and thinly sliced
- 4 scallions, trimmed and crushed
- 2–3 tbsp nam pla (fish sauce)

1 For the stock, put the water and chicken bones or crab shells in a large saucepan and bring to a boil over high heat. Reduce the heat to medium–low and add the ginger, scallions, and nam pla, then simmer for 1½ hours, or until reduced by about half, skimming off any foam. Strain the stock, discarding the solids, and remove any fat.

2 Pour the stock into a medium saucepan and bring to a gentle boil over medium heat. Reduce the heat to medium–low, then add the crabmeat and asparagus and season with salt and pepper to taste. Cover and simmer for 5 minutes, or until the flavors have blended.

3 Steadily pour the egg whites into the soup, stirring a few times, and simmer for an additional 1–2 minutes, or until fully cooked. In a ladle, stir the cornstarch and water together. Lower the ladle into the soup, then stir a few times. Cook until lightly thickened.

4 Ladle the soup into small individual bowls and scatter with the cilantro to garnish, and serve immediately.

hot & sour shrimp soup

serves 2

- 10½ oz/300 g peeled shrimp
- 2 tsp vegetable oil
- 2 fresh red chiles, sliced
- 1 garlic clove, sliced
- 3 cups fish stock
- 4 thin slices fresh ginger
- 2 lemongrass stalks, bruised
- 5 Thai lime leaves, shredded
- 2 tsp jaggery or brown sugar
- 1 tbsp chili oil
- handful of fresh cilantro leaves
- dash of lime juice

1 Dry-fry the shrimp in a skillet or wok until they turn pink. Remove and set aside.

2 Heat the vegetable oil in the same skillet, add the chiles and garlic and cook for 30 seconds.

3 Add the stock, ginger, lemongrass, Thai lime leaves, and sugar and simmer for 4 minutes. Add the reserved shrimp with the chili oil and cilantro and cook for 1 to 2 minutes.

4 Stir in the lime juice and serve immediately.

shrimp & vegetable bisque

serves 4

- 3 tbsp butter
- 1 garlic clove, chopped
- 1 onion, sliced
- 1 carrot, peeled and chopped
- 1 celery stalk, trimmed and sliced
- 5 cups fish stock
- 4 tbsp red wine
- 1 tbsp tomato paste
- 1 bay leaf
- 1 lb 5 oz/600 g shrimp, peeled and deveined
- scant ½ cup heavy cream
- salt and pepper
- light cream and whole cooked shrimp, to garnish

1 Melt the butter in a large pan over medium heat. Add the garlic and onion and cook, stirring, for 3 minutes, until slightly softened. Add the carrot and celery and cook for another 3 minutes, stirring. Pour in the stock and red wine, then add the tomato paste and bay leaf. Season to taste with salt and pepper. Bring to a boil, then lower the heat and simmer for 20 minutes. Remove from the heat and let cool for 10 minutes, then remove and discard the bay leaf.

2 Transfer half of the soup into a food processor or blender and blend until smooth. Return to the pan with the rest of the soup. Add the shrimp and cook the soup over low heat for 5–6 minutes.

3 Stir in the cream and cook for another 2 minutes, then remove from the heat and ladle into serving bowls. Garnish with swirls of light cream and whole cooked shrimp. Serve immediately.

three delicacy soup

serves 6
- 6 oz/175 g skinless, boneless chicken breast, very thinly sliced into strips
- 6 oz/175 g peeled shrimp, halved if large
- 1 tsp cornstarch
- 2 tsp water
- 1 medium egg white, lightly beaten
- 4 cups vegetable stock
- 6 oz/175 g honey-roast ham, very thinly sliced into strips
- salt
- chopped scallions or snipped fresh chives, to garnish

1 Combine the chicken and shrimp in a bowl. Mix the cornstarch to a paste with the water in another bowl and add to the mixture, together with the egg white and a pinch of salt, stirring well to coat.

2 Bring the vegetable stock to a boil in a pan over medium heat. Add the chicken mixture and the ham and bring back to a boil. Reduce the heat and simmer for 1 minute. Taste and adjust the seasoning, if necessary, and remove from the heat. Ladle into warmed bowls, garnish with scallions, and serve immediately.

tomato & smoked shellfish soup

serves 6
- 3 cups vegetable stock
- 6 ripe tomatoes, peeled, seeded, and chopped
- 1 cucumber, peeled, halved lengthwise, seeded, and chopped
- 1 shallot, chopped
- 3 tbsp sherry vinegar
- 1 tsp sugar
- 1½ tsp Dijon mustard
- ¼ tsp Tabasco sauce or pinch of cayenne pepper
- 1 lb 2 oz/500 g smoked oysters or smoked mussels
- salt and pepper
- croutons, to serve (see page 9)

1 Pour the vegetable stock into a bowl. Add the tomatoes, cucumber, shallot, vinegar, sugar, mustard, Tabasco sauce, and smoked shellfish and stir well. Season to taste with salt and pepper, cover with plastic wrap, and chill for at least 2 hours.

2 To serve, stir the soup and taste and adjust the seasoning, if necessary. Ladle into bowls, sprinkle with croutons, and serve immediately.

mussel soup

serves 6

- 36 mussels
- ⅔ cup vegetable stock
- 1¼ cups dry white wine
- ¼ onion, finely chopped
- ½ celery stalk,
  finely chopped
- 5 tbsp chopped fresh
  flat-leaf parsley
- 2½ cups heavy cream
- pinch of cayenne pepper or
  dash of Tabasco sauce
- salt and pepper
- garlic and herb bread,
  to serve

1 Scrub the mussels under cold running water and pull off the "beards." Discard any with broken shells or that do not shut immediately when sharply tapped. Put them into a large pan, pour in the vegetable stock and wine, and add the onion, celery, and parsley. Cover and bring to a boil over high heat. Cook, shaking the pan occasionally, for 3–5 minutes, until the shells have opened.

2 Remove the pan from the heat and lift out the mussels with a slotted spoon. Discard any that remain shut, shell the remainder, and set aside for another dish.

3 Strain the soup through a cheesecloth-lined strainer into a clean pan. Stir in the cream and cayenne, season to taste with salt and pepper, and let cool completely. Cover with plastic wrap and chill for at least 3 hours.

4 To serve, stir the soup and taste and adjust the seasoning, if necessary. Ladle into bowls and serve immediately with garlic and herb bread.

Index